CW01656490

The Empty Field

Also by Christine Pullein-Thompson
in Dragon Books

THE FIRST ROSETTE
THE SECOND MOUNT
THREE TO RIDE
FOR WANT OF A SADDLE
IMPOSSIBLE HORSE
THE PONY DOPERS

Christine Pullein-Thompson

The Empty Field

Illustrated

DRAGON
GRANADA PUBLISHING
London Toronto Sydney New York

Published by Granada Publishing Limited
in Dragon Books 1967
Reprinted 1970, 1973, 1976, 1977

ISBN 0 583 30056 1

First published by Burke Publishing Co Ltd 1961
This edition first published by
Atlantic Book Publishing Co Ltd 1967
Copyright © Christine Pullein-Thompson 1961

Granada Publishing Limited
Frogmore, St Albans, Herts AL2 2NF
and
3 Upper James Street, London W1R 4BP
1221 Avenue of the Americas, New York, NY 10020 USA
117 York Street, Sydney, NSW 2000, Australia
100 Skyway Avenue, Toronto, Ontario, Canada M9W 3A6
Trio City, Coventry Street, Johannesburg 2001, South Africa
CML Centre, Queen & Wyndham, Auckland 1, New Zealand

Made and printed in Great Britain by
C. Nicholls & Company Ltd
The Philips Park Press, Manchester
Siet n Intetype Plantin

This book is sold subject to the condition that it shall not, by way of trade or otherwise, be lent, re-sold, hired out or otherwise circulated without the publisher's prior consent in any form of binding or cover other than that in which it is published and without a similar condition including this condition being imposed on the subsequent purchaser.

But How?

Jocelyn and James Allcott stood staring at the three huge farm horses which were grazing on Jim Morgan's rough waste land. Behind them, the dark slag heaps raised grey heads towards the summer sky. A mile below lay the sea, calm today, lapping mildly against the rocks like a mountain lake.

The Allcotts wore jeans, open-necked shirts, sandals. Their father worked in an insurance office in the near-by town. They lived in a bungalow with a garden round it. The bungalow was bright with paint. Sometimes in the summer they would let it to a family, or would take in children as boarders. The garden, however hard they worked on it, still resembled stony pasture; the lawn was dotted with stone and rock; the concrete path was cracked and grew weeds. The wire fences sagged, so that the cows in the adjoining field were able to put their heads through and nibble the Allcotts' weeds.

Jocelyn was eleven, James twelve and a half. For years they had been known as foreigners, since they had come, in the beginning, from London. Now, at last, they were accepted. Jocelyn wore spectacles and her chestnut hair barely reached her ears; her eyes were hazel. She was a neat child. James, taller, darker, with brown eyes, was the more reckless of the two. It was he who now said, "We've got to do something. We've got to stop it happening."

"But how?"

"I don't know yet. Come on, let's hurry. We'll be late at the riding school as it is. Perhaps the gang will have some ideas."

"They are so beautiful," said Jocelyn, taking a last look at the three horses, before she hurried after her brother along the road.

"We've got to do something"

The riding school was already full of children when the Allcotts reached it. The three Fisher girls were mucking out loose boxes. Their father painted and, because of that, they never had any money. They lived in a rough stone cottage beyond the village. They were dark-haired and had blue eyes. Today, Bromwyn, the eldest, had her shirt on inside out and her toes had come through her dirty white plimsolls. Her shorts were too short and she had a smear of blue paint acros her nose. Anne, who made most of her own clothes, was tidier; she was the fattest of the three, but still slim. The youngest, Maria, who was ten, had tied her hair back with a shoelace. She had the face of an elf – thin, small-featured. They never had any money, but they were generous, and would share their sandwiches with anyone who was hungry.

People were sorry for them because their father would neither take nor keep a job. But they saw it differently. "One day Daddy will be famous," they would say, "then we're going round the world." In the holidays they were always to be found at the riding school. The proprietor, Miss Lewis, would give them a ride whenever she could, so that now they could all gallop without falling off.

Small, dark Ivor was picking out a grey pony's hoofs. He lived in one of the terrace houses in the village. His father was a miner, as was his father before him. Ivor wanted to be a jockey more than anything else in the world. His friends and relations gave him rides for Christmas and birthday presents and he did odd jobs about the village, earning money that way. Everybody liked Ivor because he was always cheerful and completely undaunted by any catastrophe. He had two grown-up sisters, one worked in the local hairdressing salon, the other was married. He was just ten but, because he was small, looked younger.

Then there was Stella, the newest member of the gang. No-one knew much about Stella. Her nose turned up at the end, and her hair appeared to be cut by her mother, for it always had a chopped look. She could ride quite well. She was always talking about a pony she had once had, called Snowball; so that Ivor was inclined to cry, "Oh, not Snowball again." Then she would blush and dry up. Her mother was a widow and worked during the day; so that in the holidays Stella spent her entire time at the riding school.

It was only recently, however, that she had been accepted into the gang.

Lastly, there was Nicholas, tall, fair, broad-shouldered, good-looking, scornful. He had a horse of his own so, officially, he shouldn't have belonged to the gang, which was otherwise horseless.

A great many children at the riding school had a pash on Nicholas who was one of the best riders in the district. If the gang had had a committee, Nicholas would have been chairman or president – he was that sort of person. He lived with his parents in a large, forbidding house. His horse, a flea-bitten grey, was called Trombone. In term-time he went to one of the larger and better-known public schools.

Nicholas had just arrived when the Allcotts reached the riding school. He stood talking to Miss Lewis. He wore jodhpurs, a shirt and tie and hacking jacket.

Miss Lewis was small; nearly forty, she was neither old nor young. She was a patient person who treated catastrophe as a natural part of life. Her hair was like pepper and salt, her eyes grey and her hands calloused by work. She was very kind.

The yard was full of Miss Lewis's pets. A lame sheep-dog sunned himself in front of the saddle-room. Guinea-fowl scratched on the midden. A puppy chewed a halter. A kitten sat purring on a horse rug.

There were seven loose boxes in the yard. Built of wood twenty years ago, when Miss Lewis had first conceived the idea of a riding school, they were now in need of paint. Their roofs were of corrugated iron, their floors of worn concrete. Beyond them was a shed where numerous ponies could be tied up. Beyond that was the granary. None of the children called Miss Lewis, Miss Lewis. To them, she was simply Audrey.

So, on this summer day, when there was hardly a ripple on the sea, not a breath of wind to stir the conifers beyond the slag heaps, when the ponies were besieged by flies and it was already too hot for energetic work, James and Jocelyn found the gang already in residence at The Sea Shore School of Equitation. That was the name Miss Lewis had given her stables twenty years ago. The name hadn't stuck. Even letters came addressed simply to "The Riding School".

James was still seeing the magnificent farm horses. He imagined them ploughing, recalled their calm eyes, the grey's wide soft nose, the bay's blaze and the dark brown's look of wisdom.

"We must save them, Jo," he told his sister.

"But how?" she repeated.

"It's no good discussing anything until the first class has gone out. Everyone's too busy now," James said.

He found a brush and started to groom a pony called Dawn. He worked slowly, his mind still with the farm horses and their proposed fate.

Jocelyn called, "Hullo," to the Fishers. "Who wants grooming?" she asked. She entered the saddle-room and looked in the diary. Most of the names were unknown to her. "They're nearly all visitors," she thought, "and every pony is booked. No hope of a ride today." She found Dawn's tack and took it out into the sunlight.

The first riders were arriving, climbing out of cars, while their parents called after them, "We'll be back in an hour. Have a good time."

"The class will be ready soon. Then, when they've gone we can begin," James said.

"Begin what?"

"Solving the problem of those poor horses, of course. Don't be such a dope."

"We may not have much time," Jocelyn said, opening Dawn's mouth with an experienced thumb and slipping the snaffle bit between her teeth.

"I know."

The riders for the first class were mounting now. The early haze had lifted from the sea. Children ran shrieking along the sands. James pulled up Dawn's webbing girths and helped up a small girl. "Shall I help you with your stirrups?" he asked.

Nicholas was holding Audrey's Periwinkle. The Fishers had already invaded the now empty loose box, armed with forks. It was a typical day at the riding school. Only James was possessed by a sense of urgency at that moment, though soon the whole gang would be involved. Audrey mounted and the class wound slowly out into the road.

"I wish I was going too," Ivor said.

Everyone was assembled now in the granary, which smelt of hay and oats and long-forgotten apples.

"Well, fire away. What is all this about?" asked Nicholas impatiently.

"It's like this," James began. "You've probably all seen the shire horses in Jim Morgan's field. Well, they're going to be shipped to Ireland soon and, from there, well, you know where they will go."

"You mean on one of those ghastly boats to France?" cried Bromwyn.

"And then on the sealed trains to the slaughterhouses," James added. "I think we ought to save them. Jo and I have looked at their teeth. They're not very old. The brown's quite young, in fact; only four or five."

"But you can't just ship horses to Ireland. I'm sure you can't. They have to be worth more than so much," Nicholas said.

"Well, perhaps Jim Morgan has some arrangements with someone."

"They're so beautiful. Have you seen them, Anne?" Jocelyn asked.

"They've probably got the story wrong," thought Nicholas, picking hayseeds off his nylon socks. But now Bromwyn was speaking. She had climbed on to a bale of hay. Nicholas thought she looked rather ridiculous.

"We must buy the horses," she announced. Everyone was a little surprised, mostly that such a suggestion should come from one of the Fishers, who lived a hand-to-mouth existence.

"We must raise the money," she continued. "I've seen the horses. They are like a piece of dying England. They should be preserved by the National Trust."

"Hear, hear," cried James.

"Supposing we go and see old Jim Morgan and hear his story," suggested Nicholas. "Aren't we rather rushing our fences?"

"He'll tell a lot of lies. He's as slippery as an eel. We should know. He's our nearest neighbour," James replied.

"Well, how do you know that they are going to Ireland, then?" Nicholas asked.

"We heard him selling them," Jocelyn said.

"We're not fools," said James now angrily. "We know Jim Morgan. He's out for what he can get."

"He ought to be in prison," announced Maria.

"We must open a fund. Can't we have a sale and each send something? I've got a new skirt. I made it for myself, but by the time it was finished I'd grown fatter. It must be worth ten shillings," said Anne.

"Which isn't much when we probably need £150," Nicholas answered.

"It's a super idea all the same. Jo and I have got several books we hate and there's some new shoes of Mummy's which don't fit," James said.

"I could do the posters," Bromwyn offered.

"I could make some sweets," Stella said.

"We'd better run something else as well. What about

a dog gymkhana. I went to one once. It was smashing," Ivor said. He was thinking, "Grandfather would have approved of this." Until he died, his grandfather had sat in the chimney corner, talking about the old days when ponies had worked in the pits. "There's nothing like a pony. The pits have never been the same since they started using machines. They're better than a friend," he had said. He'd had a favourite called Polly. "Yes, Grandfather would have approved," thought Ivor again, and he imagined his father's greyhound winning the flat race at the dog gymkhana.

"But how long have we got to raise the money?" asked Nicholas.

"We don't know," said James and was suddenly obsessed by gloom. "It will take at least a week to organise anything at all and, even then, we may only earn twenty pounds. That wouldn't buy one shire horse, much less three," he thought despondently.

"Perhaps we can borrow money from a moneylender or something," Bromwyn said.

"Not likely. We're not old enough to borrow money," James said.

Jocelyn had been writing everything down. Her ambition was to be a secretary, perhaps on a farm where she could keep her own horse. "Suggestions so far: (1) that we should see Jim Morgan, (2) hold a sale, (3) hold a dog gymkhana," she announced, consulting her notebook.

"Supposing we see Jim Morgan first and see how much time we've got," suggested Nicholas, standing up. James realised then that Nicholas was with them. His despondency lifted. "With Nicholas to help," he decided, "anything could be achieved."

"Who will come with me?" Nicholas asked. "Two of us will be enough."

"I'm not tidy enough," Bromwyn said, looking at her plimsolls.

"If you put your shirt on the right way, you'll be all

right. We're the eldest after all. James and Jocelyn had better stay away, if they know him already," Nicholas said.

Bromwyn hurried to the saddle-room, took her shirt off, turned it inside out and put it on again. "Anyone got a comb?" she called.

Jocelyn had a pink one, which broke in Bromwyn's hair.

"Come on, your hair doesn't matter," called Nicholas.

They set off in the sunlight; soon they could hear the sea. "I wish I was tidier," thought Bromwyn. "I never even have a comb to my name."

"We must think how to begin. Any ideas?" asked Nicholas. He liked Bromwyn, though he couldn't have said why. "The dog gymkhana's a good idea. But we do need time," he added.

It wasn't far to Jim Morgan's ramshackle place. The three shire horses stood by an empty water trough, their lips drooping, their eyes half closed against the flies which swarmed round their heads. Mrs. Morgan was digging in the garden. A pointer lay by the wooden shack the Morgans called their house.

"Is Mr. Morgan at home?" Nicholas called. The digging woman raised her head and nodded towards the shack.

"Here goes," said Nicholas.

Making Plans

They found him in the small kitchen at the back, in his shirt sleeves with his braces hanging down. He was small, with eyes which were both mean and cunning and a few stained teeth. He wore a cap on the back of his head. "Good afternoon," he said. His voice had a wheedle in it like a gypsy's voice.

"He looks slippery enough," thought Nicholas.

"We came about the horses. We're interested in them. Are they for sale by any chance?" Nicholas asked.

"You mean the shire horses? But they're no good to you."

"Are they, or are they not for sale?" demanded Nicholas.

"They're sold, but that doesn't mean I'm not open to a good offer. They're good horses."

"We can see that. What will you take?"

"What, for the three?"

"Yes."

"Nicholas is being too much of the bully," thought Bromwyn. "You can't bully men like Jim Morgan."

"What do you offer?"

"I don't offer anything. I'm asking your price," Nicholas retorted.

"I'd take two hundred for the three."

"That's ridiculous," Nicholas cried.

"I've told you they're already sold," said Jim Morgan, retreating a pace into the kitchen.

"He's going to shut the door in a minute," thought Bromwyn, "slam it in our faces. Everything will be over then."

"When do they go?" she cried.

"In ten days. Two 'undred, and that's my last word."

"We'll come and see you again in a few days," Nicholas said.

"Good afternoon," Jim Morgan shut the door.

"Swine," muttered Nicholas. "I wouldn't trust him with sixpence."

They walked back along the path. Mrs. Morgan was still digging and didn't raise her head. "I bet she has an awful life," Nicholas said.

"Ten days. It's not much time," Bromwyn said.

"I wonder how long he's been doing this," Nicholas said.

"I don't know. I hate him anyway."

"The dog gymkhana's not a bad idea. Perhaps we can

run it for ponies too. Then the holiday crowd might come in, the Mums and Dads to watch their children ride."

"Anne would make the rosettes. She's awfully good at sewing."

"It could be a bit of everything. It had better be next Saturday. That gives us a week," Nicholas said.

"It's hardly long enough."

"But what about the prizes?"

"People will have to give them. I've got a cup I won for swimming. I can have my name taken off. We can say it's in aid of Unwanted Horses." Nicholas felt full of enthusiasm now. At first he had been sceptical. Now he was ready to fight for the three horses, to give up everything else until they were saved.

They could see the riding school, with the class approaching the gate and Ivor standing outside with Maria.

"We haven't achieved much," thought Bromwyn. But we do know now how much money we need; that, at least, is something . . ."

They met again in the granary and nobody made any speeches. Nicholas said simply, "We've got ten days in which to raise two hundred pounds. Jim Morgan won't take any less."

"That's fifty more than the slaughter-house man offered," gasped James, while Jocelyn wrote the sum down in her notebook, put a dash and added ten days.

"I'd like to pull his shack down," shouted Maria.

"We thought we'd hold a dog and pony gymkhana combined next Saturday," Bromwyn said. "And a rummage sale and anything else anyone can think of."

"If I can borrow a pony, I'll give pony rides at sixpence a time," Ivor said.

"I'll do the posters tonight," Bromwyn offered.

"We're too late for publication in the local paper," Nicholas said.

They started to decide the classes. When they had finished, the schedule ran like this:

Class One, Handy Pony Competition, riders under ten.
Class Two, Handy Hunter Competition, riders ten and over but under sixteen.
Class Three, Jumping for ponies under 13.2, riders under ten.

Class Four, Jumping for ponies not exceeding 14.2, riders under sixteen.
Class Five, Bending Race, Open.
Class Six, Apple and Bucket race, Open.
Class Seven, Musical Poles, Open.
Class Eight, Potato race, Open.

"Now we have to think of the snags," Nicholas said when Jocelyn had written the classes down.

"And the time we begin," Anne said.

"And the prizes; what about them? We can't afford to give much," Ivor added.

"They must come out of the entrance fees," James answered.

"Jocelyn had better be secretary. Any one against? Passed and carried," Nicholas chanted.

"And James had better look after the money," Ivor said.

"I'll borrow Daddy's typewriter and get some copies done by the morning for everyone's approval or disapproval," Jocelyn said. "What time will it start?"

"Eleven o'clock," Nicholas said.

"What about judges?" Anne asked.

"My father might be one. He was in a cavalry regiment. He's got a stop watch which will be useful and I'll get him to mug up the jumping rules."

"Perhaps Audrey can suggest someone as a co-judge."

"Where are the jumps coming from?" Jocelyn asked.

"I don't know. But I'll try and solve that one," Nicholas offered.

"The entrance fee had better be five shillings," Jocelyn

said. "Otherwise how will we ever make enough?"

"That's too much for the competitions. They'd better be two and sixpence."

"You mean for all but the Jumping and Handy Pony competitions?" Jocelyn asked Nicholas.

"That's right."

"Shall I write out a Dog Gymkhana programme?" asked Ivor.

"O.K." James said.

"I'm going to run the White Elephant Stall. They generally make pounds," Anne said.

"We'll meet again tomorrow at eight, shall we?" Nicholas asked, standing up. He was by far the tallest. Ivor always felt small in comparison; but he consoled himself, thinking, "Nicholas could never be a jockey, even if he wanted to be more than anything else in the world."

The second class had gone out without their help. The stable yard was quiet and empty; the loose-box doors stood open. The clock in the saddle-room told James that it was ten to twelve. Everything was the same but somehow different. Even in the quietness of the yard, he still felt the sense of urgency which he knew would possess him until the horses were either saved or sent for slaughter.

"But we haven't decided where to hold it," he cried.

"In the paddock at my place," Nicholas said.

Stella had hardly spoken. "I'll make some cakes for your stall, Anne," she offered.

"Thank you very much. If you've got any old clothes, bring them too – anything."

Bromwyn was seeing the posters already in her mind. She started to run, out of the yard, down the dusty road to the right, and along the track which led home.

"I'm staying for a bit. Are you?" Maria asked Stella.

Nicholas was already on his way home, ticking things off in his mind. Jumps, ring ropes, judges, prizes. As usual, he had undertaken too much.

Jocelyn and James stopped to look at the three shires again on their way home.

Their mother wasn't expecting them home so soon.

"What's happened? I thought you were having lunch at the stables. I haven't cooked anything . . ." she said in a worried voice. She was like that, always harassed, as though she carried the weight of the world on her shoulders.

"We've got a new lodger, an American girl," she said.

"Oh, no," cried James.

"She rides. She's coming in time for tea. Her parents have gone down with something or other . . ."

"What's she like?" asked Jocelyn.

"I don't know. Doctor James telephoned. They've been up at the big hotel on holiday. Poor kid, be nice to her . . ."

"Those old shoes of yours, the ones which don't fit, can we have them?" James asked.

"Whatever for? They're not old. I only wore them once."

"For a rummage sale," Jocelyn said.

James untied his packet of sandwiches. "I hope the American girl isn't miserable all the time. We've got an awful lot on," he said. He started to do sums in his head. How many entries would they need for a first prize of a guinea? They'd better just put *cash prizes* on the schedule, he decided; that way they could adjust the prizes to the number of competitors; it would be the fairest way, too. Like his father, he had a head for figures; but, however many sums he did, he couldn't see their gymkhana, fête, whatever they called it, raising two hundred pounds. It wasn't a thing which happened; or only in dreams.

"Thank you, Mummy," Jocelyn said, still thinking about shoes. "Have you any other things you don't want? James and I thought we might take some of our books along." She wrote in her notebook, *White Elephant Stall* and, under it, *Shoes*. "They're sure to fetch five shillings," thought Jocelyn.

"Will you girls sew the rosettes for the Dog Gymkhana? They needn't be very good," Ivor asked Maria and Stella. "Anne can't do them all, can she?"

"I'm so bad at sewing," grumbled Maria.

"I'll do them," Stella said.

"I'll get off home now then," Ivor said. "I'll let you know how many when I've got the schedule worked out. It'll take a bit of time, writing and spelling not being my strong point."

He walked across the sands, kicking at seaweed, throwing a pebble at the retreating sea. Then he climbed upwards to reach the terrace cottage where he lived. The road was hot under his feet and the hot sun was beating against the thick flannel shirt he wore. "I could do with a bike," he thought, "but there's no hope of that now. Oh well, horses are more important than machines." He went round the back way, where the washing hung and the dustbin stood and his father's sweet peas bloomed prim and pastel in straight rows.

"I'm back, Mum," he called. But the cottage was empty. Ivor started to search for pen and pencil. "If we don't save those poor horses, who will?" he wondered.

Ruth

As expected, the American girl arrived in time for tea. She wore what she called sneakers, bobby socks and a loud checked shirt outside her jeans. Her hair was straight, brown and held back by a slide.

"Hiya. I came by cab," she cried, walking up the stony front path swinging a hold-all.

Jocelyn was typing in the front room at her father's desk. The telephone stood on the brown window-ledge. It was her third draft copy of the schedule and, like the previous two, it was full of mistakes.

"Perhaps she can type," she thought hopefully, going to the door. "Hiya, I'm Ruth," the American said.

She was taller than Jocelyn and full of self assurance, as though she imagined the whole world her friend. "I've brought you some candy," she cried, seeing Mrs. Allcott for the first time.

"She looks nice," thought James, coming in from the garden, "not a townee at any rate."

"These are my children, James and Jocelyn," Mrs. Allcott said.

"Hiya," Ruth said again.

"I expect you'd like to see your room. Take her along, Joyce, will you?" asked Mrs. Allcott.

James followed. "Do you ride by any chance?" he asked.

"Sure."

"And type?"

"Sure, with one finger," laughed Ruth.

"She's too good to be true," thought Jocelyn, saying, "Here's your room. I hope you like it. You can see the sea. Follow me and I'll show you the bathroom."

James said, "I'll get you some towels and soap. I hope you *do* really like riding, because we spend all our time at the riding school. It's quite near."

"See those three cart horses out of the bathroom window?" asked Jocelyn. "We're trying to save them from being eaten. We've got to raise two hundred pounds in ten days. You can imagine what that's like."

"How many dollars is that?"

"I don't know; but it's a lot in English money."

"But heck, you don't eat horses, do you?" cried Ruth.

"No, but the French do."

Ruth washed her hands. "We don't have tea back home," she said, following Jocelyn along the passage.

"Daddy's home," James called. "He wants to know what you're typing, Jo."

After tea, the two children took Ruth into the garden and, sitting on the edge of the rockery, told her about their plans. Her remarks were enthusiastic; at least, they judged them so. She stood staring at the shire horses for a long time.

"We've got two like that on the farm back home, called Pat and Pep," she said at last.

Nicholas rode Trombone home. His father was relaxing after a game of golf; his mother was wiping out the dishwasher in the high Victorian kitchen.

"You've had lunch, haven't you?" she asked.

"Yes, I ate my sandwiches on the way here," replied Nicholas leading Trombone into the kitchen.

"Is there any sugar anywhere?" he asked, searching the kitchen cupboard, Trombone's reins over his arm.

He turned his mare out and, watching her roll, thought, "Well, it's now or never." He had a funny feeling in the pit of his stomach. He could only pray that his father was in a good mood. His mother wouldn't mind so much, since she was always behind Nicholas in everything. He wandered round to the front of the house. Sunlight played on the sloping lawn. A boxer dog lay at his father's feet.

"Well, Nick, what is it?" asked Captain Owen.

There was a deck-chair which Nicholas sank into.

"I was wondering whether we could hold a gymkhana, just a little affair, in the paddock next Saturday; whether you would judge it, or help judge it." He felt that he was jumping his fences too quickly, yet he had to say it all, get it over. "Several of us are running it. We want to raise some money to save some horses. There isn't much time."

Nicholas was standing up now, running his hands through his fair hair. "I should have put it better," he kept thinking. And, of course, his father started to light his pipe as he always did before reaching a decision, slowly, without saying a word. "I've more or less promised the paddock," said Nicholas desperately. "Some girls are doing the posters and sewing the rosettes. If it isn't all right I must let them know at once."

"I suppose it's all right. It'll make a mess, of course. The cars will have to park further down the road. Perhaps Mr. Jones will let you have his yard for a park, he's a good chap."

Nicholas said, "Thank you."

"Are you having jumping classes?" asked Captain Owen. Nicholas started to explain. It took a long time. By the time he had finished Mrs. Owen was there, sitting in the other deck-chair with her knitting.

"I'm glad you're trying to save the horses," she said.

"Old Johnnie Smith has a set of jumps. Why don't you ring him?" asked Captain Owen. "What about Watchman, is he eligible for the Dog Gymkhana?" he added, prodding the boxer with his foot.

"I'll find some things for Anne's stall. I always have liked Anne, she seems such a sensible girl," said Mrs. Owen.

Nicholas hurried indoors, found Johnnie Smith's telephone number and rang him up. It all seemed too easy, ridiculously easy. Johnnie Smith promised his jumps at once, even offered to bring them over in his horse-box. Nicholas rang off feeling worried. "Things shouldn't be so easy," he thought, "easy come, easy go."

The sunlight was fading when he went outside again; his parents still sat in the deck-chairs. Trombone was under the trees by the water trough. "It's okay. Any idea for another judge?" he asked.

His father was still smoking. Nicholas couldn't unwind. "There must be someone," he said.

In the end, they remembered Miss Prickett, an ex-Master of Foxhounds. Nicholas returned to the telephone. When he got through to her house he had to wait, since she was said to be in the stables.

At last he was speaking to Miss Prickett. "Of course, it's short notice but luckily I'm not doing anything next Saturday. Where did you say you live?"

Nicholas gave her most of the details.

"I'll come. Eleven o'clock is it? I won't let you down."

"Another hurdle cleared," thought Nicholas, returning to his parents. They could hear laughter coming up from the sea shore.

"It's only the ring ropes now," Nicholas said.

"You can hire them from the rope shop in Johnstown," replied his father.

"What about the posts?"

"Try the Council. They've got some iron ones down at the dump."

Nicholas started to whistle then. He saw himself announcing everything settled when he arrived at the riding school in the morning. The whole gang would be pleased. They would be able to put up the posters straight away. Perhaps, if the gymkhana was a success, they could hold the same sort of thing every year. "The village needs waking up," decided Nicholas. "There's never anything on here besides the eternal Whist Drive."

Bromwyn had painted three posters. They were bright and large. One said:

ARE YOU COMING?
DOG AND PONY GYMKHANA.
SATURDAY AUGUST 12TH 11 A.M.
AT THE OLD MANSE BY KIND PERMISSION OF
CAPTAIN OWEN
RUMMAGE STALL. PRIZES.
ADMISSION 1/- CHILDREN HALF PRICE.

Below the writing, a grey horse jumped across the poster. In one corner there was a table covered with oddments. Another poster simply said:

WHITE ELEPHANT STALL

THE OLD MANSE

SATURDAY 11 A.M.

and round the outside there ran a line of hats of all shapes and sizes.

"People always go for hats," Bromwyn told Anne.

"But we haven't got any for my stall. We can't make people come under false pretences," Anne retorted.

"We must get some then. I'm not going to throw away the poster. It's the best to date."

Anne was knitting. She had finished one baby sock already. Luckily their father was out painting somewhere in the hills so they had the run of his disreputable studio. Bromwyn started another poster.

"Ivor wanted me to do the Dog Gymkhana rosettes. Me of all people!" exclaimed Maria, coming in. "I've had a lovely afternoon. You should have stayed; three people didn't turn up. I had Meadowsweet for a whole hour and we jumped."

"Don't, you're making my mouth water. I shall dribble on the poster," Bromwyn said.

"I wish they were riding horses. Then we could keep them," Maria said.

"But where? Anyway we can't even afford shoes for horses, much less food. You can't hold things in aid of yourself," Anne said.

"She's like that," Maria thought. "Always wants to do the right thing. I'm more like Daddy." She sat on the table and swung her legs. "Why don't you go out and see if anyone will give you some old hats for Anne's stall?" Bromwyn suggested.

"Hats, who wants hats?"

"Everybody," replied Bromwyn firmly. "The rest of the posters will have to be done on cardboard in Indian ink. I've used up all the poster paint," she continued. "What a bore, I hate lettering."

"We must stick them up early. Then people will see them on their way to church," Anne said.

Mr. Fisher's figure blotted out the sunlit doorway. "What are you doing in here?" he asked.

They jumped up guiltily and, all at once, started to explain. When they had finished, Mr. Fisher said, "You can have some of my canvases, see if you can sell them on a twenty per cent. commission. Isn't tea ready yet? I'm hungry."

"Bags not get tea," cried Maria, disappearing in search of hats.

"I must finish this sock. I've only got one more line," Anne muttered.

Bromwyn went into the small back kitchen and lit the Calor gas. She could see her mother coming up the path, now laden with shopping baskets. Mrs. Fisher wore her hair long, with a fringe in front. There were tired lines round her brown eyes. Her shoulders stooped under the weight of the shopping.

"Why didn't you tell us to get some of it?" cried Bromwyn going out to meet her.

Stella reached the town as the shops were closing. She had one and sixpence in her pocket with which she bought three yards of red ribbon. "You'll need canvas backing or a round piece of cardboard if it's for rosettes," the shop assistant said.

When Stella reached the flat her mother was home already.

"Hullo, darling," she called. "Did you have a good day?"

"Super, thank you. I rode all afternoon. Audrey says my leg position has improved enormously," Stella said.

She ran round the kitchen pretending to be a horse. "I'm helping to run a Dog and Pony Gymkhana. It's to be next Saturday in Nicholas's field." For the first time she felt that she really belonged to the gang. "Will you be able to come, Mummy? I'm making the rosettes for

"I'm not going to throw away the poster – it's the best to date"

the dog part of it. Look, I've got some ribbon already."

She tore, bucking, round the kitchen. "I'm chestnut and called Thunderbolt," she cried.

"I'll help you with the rosettes and I'll try to get next Saturday off," her mother promised, pouring water into the teapot.

Stella started to tell her mother about the three horses. She wished now that she had seen them.

"What will you do with them when you *have* bought them?" asked her mother.

"I don't know. Give them to the zoo or something I suppose. But we haven't got them yet. I wish we had a dog," Stella said.

"It wouldn't have much of a life when you're at school, would it?"

"No," admitted Stella, thinking how empty the flat was. "If it wasn't for the riding school I'd be bored stiff," she thought.

"Perhaps we could get you a guinea-pig or hamsters or some mice."

But Stella didn't want them. She wanted a pony, a dog, a garden full of flowers.

"I said I would make some things for Anne Fisher's stall too," she told her mother, who stood, small and neat, without a hair out of place. She was fair like Stella, with grey eyes. She was emptying lumps of sugar into a glass dish from Woolworths.

Ivor had worked out the Dog Gymkhana schedule at last. The kettle hummed softly on the old black range, cups and saucers were grouped together on the oilcloth on the table.

"That's it, Mum," he said.

"Class 1. Dog in the Best Condition
Class 2. Best Tricks
Class 3. Flat Race
Class 4. Jumping for Dogs under 24 inches

Class 5. Jumping, Open

Class 6. Consolation Race.

Class 6, that's for dogs which haven't won anything. It'll be a surprise. It'll be sixpence to enter and the prizes will be for the dogs," he added. He had covered his face in ink.

"It sounds all right. You'd better wash. There's some hot water in the kettle." His mother's hair was knotted into a bun. She wore felt slippers and a flowered pinafore.

"Dad should be back from the football match in a minute or two. We'd better wait," she added.

Washing his hands in the enamel bowl in the cracked sink, Ivor was seeing the horses again. He was certain now that they would save them. With Nicholas, he felt they couldn't fail.

"Dreaming again?" his mother asked.

Ivor dried his hands. "I should think old Pete would win the flat race," he said, patting the greyhound which lay under the table. His father was home now, hanging up his cap on the back of the door.

"They won," he said, "Three nil. The home team won. Do you hear that, boy? Don't you care for football? Wouldn't you like to come with me next Saturday?"

"I want to be a jockey. 'I'm too small for football," Ivor said, sitting down at the table, picking up a slice of bread and butter. "Anyway I'm helping to run a gymkhana and fête at the Old Manse next Saturday, at Captain Owen's place."

"It's the horses he likes, isn't it, Ivor?" asked his mother.

"That's it. I'm like Grandad," Ivor said.

What About That Grey?

They met once more in the granary and the Allcotts brought Ruth, not without trepidation. She found the stable yard cute, the ponies small, the smell the same as it was back home.

Nicholas had ridden over on Trombone; on the way, he had stopped to see Mr. Jones about the car park in his yard. Once again Nicholas had been lucky, so that now he felt jubilant, extremely competent, the sort of person who gets things done. "When I'm grown up I shall be a business executive. My factory will run like clockwork; I shall travel all over the world, and be rich enough to have a farm and horses to come home to," he thought, whistling as he climbed the granary's rickety ladder.

Stella had two sample rosettes in her pocket. She had arrived on the 7 a.m. bus and had already ridden a pony up from the lower meadow, emptied three wheelbarrows and groomed Meadowsweet. Bromwyn was laden with posters. Anne had a list of questions stuffed in her pocket. Maria felt guilty for, except for collecting three hats for her sister's stall, she had done nothing at all.

Ivor was the last to arrive. He had walked the long way round because he had wanted to visit the shire horses. Audrey called, "Whatever are you lot up to?" when she saw them assembled in the granary again.

"We'll tell you later," Nicholas called back, climbing on to a bale of hay, looking at Ruth and wondering what she was like, whether she would be any use, or just a hindrance to them all.

He said, "Shall I speak first?" and, without waiting for an answer, began: "I've got the judges, the jumps, the paddock and a car park." He couldn't keep a note of triumph out of his voice. They expected him to get things done and he had. "I know where the ring ropes are coming from and the stakes. Daddy has offered the loan of five pounds to cover expenses, without interest, of course."

Ivor looked at Nicholas with admiration. His contribution was so small in comparison, just the crumpled piece of paper in his pocket. He wondered if the others would even be able to read his writing.

Jocelyn passed round the typed schedule. "Ruth did most of it," she said.

"Of course, there's lots more to do. But I've broken the back of it," Nicholas said.

Ruth liked Nicholas already. She was like that, could always make up her mind about people in a moment.

"Here are the posters," Bromwyn said. Last night they had seemed masterpieces but today, in the morning light, they appeared quite different. Bromwyn could see all their faults – the grey horse's legs were out of proportion, for instance, and there was a smudge on some of the lettering.

"Good heavens! You can paint. Are you an artist or something?" exclaimed Ruth.

"Daddy is," Bromwyn said. She wondered what Nicholas would say; probably he liked neat posters like the ones which advertised the local whist drives.

"Smashing!" exclaimed Ivor.

"We'd better get them up right away," Nicholas said.

"Here's the Dog Gymkhana schedule," Ivor said, pulling the piece of paper from his pocket.

It was much cooler. There was a breeze coming up from the sea. Small clouds chased each other across a grey-blue sky.

A few minutes later, they started to leave the granary.

"Do you think I can ride in the gymkhana?" asked Ruth.

Now Stella managed to say what she had been trying to all the time they had been in the granary. Her mother worked in an office.

"Mummy says she'll roneo all the schedules if you like. She'll only charge for the paper," she announced.

Someone cheered, while Jocelyn and Ivor handed over their schedules. "Ask her to be as quick as possible. We ought to have sent them to the horsey people long ago," Nicholas said.

"If you let me have a list of addresses, I'll send them off as soon as they're done. That'll be tomorrow evening," offered Stella.

"What about money for stamps?"

"I'll keep an expense account," Stella replied. The others were surprised. They seemed to be seeing Stella for the first time. "Of course, her mother's a secretary," remembered Nicholas.

Ruth was trying to book a horse. "I'd like one for the gymkhana too," she told Audrey who, by now, had heard all about it.

"I don't know about that. We have to give our regular pupils first chance," said Audrey. "I'll let you know."

"I can ride all right. I've got my own mare back home," Ruth answered. She looked round the yard and her eye was caught by Trombone. "What about that grey? She'd suit me all right. Daddy will pay anything you ask. He'll be out of the nursing home by Saturday," she said. She was one of those people who won't take "No" for an answer; being an only child, more often than not she had her own way.

"She's not mine," replied Audrey, going into the saddle-room. "She's Nicholas's and he certainly won't hire her to anyone."

"We'll see about that," thought Ruth.

Meanwhile, Nicholas and Bromwyn were sticking up the posters.

"What do you think of Ruth? She's not bad looking, is she?" Nicholas asked.

"I'm not much good at judging people. She seems awfully old for her age but then, Americans generally are, aren't they?" Bromwyn asked.

People were coming home from early services. They stopped to read the posters, stood and stared, murmured "Saturday," and walked on again. Visitors were arriving in cars, with picnic cases, prams, tents, suitcases stuffed into boots or piled on luggage racks. "It doesn't feel like Sunday somehow. I generally get up late, that's why, I suppose," Nicholas said.

The posters were looking more professional now that they were up. "We'd better hurry back and make out a list of addresses," said Nicholas when all of them were up.

"Have you thought any more about prizes?" Bromwyn asked.

"Not really, but I was thinking we might ask the saddler to give us something and Johns, the corn merchants."

"That's a good idea. I suppose if we don't raise two hundred pounds we'll buy two horses instead of three, but what agony it will be deciding which."

"It'll have to be a matter of age."

"I suppose so, though Jim Morgan is sure to want us to have the smallest – the ones with the least meat on them. Ugh," Bromwyn said.

"I wonder where he sends them from. I'm sure it's all fearfully illegal. He looks dishonest," Nicholas replied. They were back now in the stable yard. Ivor was mounting a black pony called Ivanhoe, his face just one large smile.

"I'm giving him a spot of exercise before the class goes out," he called.

Ruth was grooming Trombone. "Hiya," she called.

"The cheek of it," Bromwyn thought. But Nicholas said nothing, only walked whistling into the saddle-room to search for a pencil and paper, so that he could begin his list of addresses.

The Allcotts were saddling ponies, avoiding everyone, because they were embarrassed by Ruth's behaviour.

"I don't know why we have to take paying guests," muttered James angrily.

"It's Mummy's pocket money and it pays for our riding lessons," Jocelyn answered.

"But she's using a curry comb on Trombone of all horses," exclaimed James. He felt deeply ashamed. "It's like climbing up a mountain roped all wrong or riding with a twisted girth," he thought furiously.

"She'll get kicked in a moment," Jocelyn said.

"You can trot him over the cavaletti, Ivor," Audrey called.

Ivor rode in a dream; the house where he lived was another world. This was where he belonged, with the creak of leather, the clink of bit and stirrup, the smell of horse and the neat mane in front, the paddock full of jumps, the language of horsemanship. They were all, somehow, part of him, so that they alone brought him alive, turned him into someone with prospects, with a future. He loved Ivanhoe; the pony was quiet without being sluggish and they seemed to understand one another, so arguments between them were very rare. "If only you were mine," Ivor thought, entering the paddock and leaning down to pat the black neck in front of him.

"I've got to catch the twelve o'clock bus home," Stella told Maria. "We always have a large lunch on Sundays. It's really the only big meal Mummy and I ever have together. Ivor thinks the rosettes are all right."

"I'm collecting for Anne's stall, hats mostly," said Maria quickly, for she didn't want to be asked to make rosettes again.

Nicholas came across to Stella. "Here are some addresses. Can you read my writing?" he asked.

"Yes. I shall be able to address the envelopes tonight then," Stella said.

"I'm sure to think of some more addresses and I haven't consulted Audrey yet; so I'll do some, too, ready for the schedules when you bring them," Nicholas said.

He was staring at Ruth now, wondering how to say, "Don't use a curry comb on my mare," without sounding rude. He moved away across the yard. He thought, "One shouldn't be rude to foreigners and Americans are really foreigners, whatever you like to say." He wanted Ruth to like him, to go home reflecting that English people have beautiful manners and are some of the nicest people in the world.

James was still afflicted by a sense of urgency. Nothing was being done fast enough. He carried a mass of figures in his head and, at the top of the column, there was the outstanding sum of two hundred pounds. It was written there like an unpaid debt; in his more optimistic moments it was a challenge, too, something to be found in nine days, something almost impossible to be accomplished by hard work or a miracle. The horses were there, too, in his imagination, standing by the water trough, their long lower lips drooping, their eyes complacent, patient, completely unsuspecting.

"And Ruth is no asset," he thought angrily, watching her with Nicholas. He saw that they were the same height, though she was three years the younger. They were talking about Trombone. She was pointing at the grey mare's legs, laughing. "Americans have everything," thought James with anger, "money, horses, cars, whatever they want. She even thinks she can have Trombone!"

"Cheer up," said Audrey in passing. "Would you like a ride on Patchwork? He's free at eleven."

"Yes, please. Thank you."

The ride would shake him out of his ill humour. For a whole hour he would be able to forget the three shire horses and wouldn't feel responsible for Ruth. James started to smile, his brow cleared.

"I'm going to ride at eleven," he called to Jocelyn.

The ten o'clock class was going out now; the day was warming up, so that once again there seemed hardly a breath of air in the stable yard. Nicholas was still talking

"Don't use a curry comb on my mare"

to Ruth. "Perhaps your curry combs are different," he suggested.

"Yes, they are, they're rubber," Ruth answered. She returned to the topic she wouldn't leave alone. She worried it as a dog does a bone. "But if you're not riding Trombone on Saturday, if you can't as you darn well say, why can't you hire her to me? Daddy will pay. He'll pay thirty dollars, for sure. That's ten of your British pounds I guess. If *you* don't want it, what about those horses you want to save?"

Her eyes never left his face. She knew he was wavering. "I don't know what to say. I'll think about it," replied Nicholas at last. The thought of the ten pounds was on his conscience now. For the sake of the shire horses he would say 'Yes' – he knew that. It was before him in black and white, in capital letters. But before him, too, was Trombone. She had been schooled by a dressage expert; she had cost his father a lot of money. Did Ruth know anything about correct aids, let alone dressage? He couldn't bear the thought of her hauling Trombone round, kicking her wildly at jumps.

"I'd like to see you ride first," he said. That sounded conceited, as though he thought Americans couldn't ride as well as the English.

"Sure. But when can I ride her?"

"I meant on one of Audrey's horses."

"You don't think I ride well enough. That's it." Now Ruth was angry. "You think Americans can't ride. Well, I'm a Virginian."

"I'm sure you can ride, much better than me in fact. I'm not very good. Only Trombone's in training for all sorts of things and I don't want her muddled just now, that's all."

Nicholas felt far too hot. He snatched off his jersey.

"Can't we leave it for a time? There's so much to do. I've got to clear up the paddock this afternoon. It's full of thistles," he said. James had been listening and he called, "I'll help you."

"Tomorrow I've got to hire the ropes and posts. And there's still the prizes to think about." The yard was empty now; the class had gone; only the gang and Ruth remained.

"I want some wood for the Dog Gymkhana jumps," Ivor said.

"We've got some laths; they'll be just the job," Nicholas replied.

"What about some of Daddy's old canvases for a wall? We can paint over the pictures," suggested Maria.

The gang were together again. Ruth stood feeling shut out. "Daddy will give a prize I guess. He gives them back home," she said.

"Everybody who can, come to my place this afternoon then. We'll have a working party," Nicholas said. "I hope to have the jumps over tomorrow. There's a lot of posters for you to do, Bromwyn, signs rather. You know – CAR PARK, LADIES, COLLECTING RING, and so on."

"Shall I be at the gate on the day? I don't mind taking money and selling tickets," James said.

"Nicholas had better be collecting-ring steward and Jocelyn and Stella can be in the secretary's tent," suggested Ivor.

"We need a general liaison officer. What about you, Bromwyn?" Nicholas asked.

"If you think I'm competent enough. I can't add up," Bromwyn answered.

"But you can talk intelligently to the judges. You can't expect me to manage my father. He won't do anything I say," replied Nicholas with a laugh.

James was beginning to feel better every moment. They seemed to be getting somewhere, at last. For the first time, he imagined crowds; horses jumping in a ring, cheers, judges on shooting sticks, counting the money afterwards. "If only we make enough," he thought. "Two hundred pounds. It's like a fortune, yet really it isn't much, not enough to buy a new car. The happiness of three horses is cheap at the price. Why aren't some of us rich, really rich?" he wondered.

"Daddy will give a prize," Ruth announced again.

"Oh, thanks," replied Nicholas in an absent-minded voice. Then he turned back to Bromwyn; "If you do a few more posters tonight, I'll take them in to Johnstown in the morning. I'll bike to your place about seven. O.K.?" he continued.

"Yes. All right. But I hope we'll be up."

"Just put them outside the door. It's not going to rain."

"They won't be in poster paint."

"Never mind."

James felt like singing now. In a moment the ride would be back. "Will you look after Ruth?" he asked Jocelyn.

A moment later they could hear hoofs coming along the road. Nicholas said, "I must be off," fetched his mare, mounted, called, "See you all after lunch," and rode off.

The class came in. "The eleven o'clock ride is in the paddock," Audrey announced dismounting from her chestnut, Flashlight.

Everything was the same as usual except for a vague air of excitement which hung over the yard. A stranger coming in would have thought, "Something is in the air," without knowing what. Audrey could feel it. "Oh Lord, I mustn't book up any rides for next Saturday," she thought. "However shall I remember?"

As Crooked as a Twisted Nail

Riding home, Nicholas thought about Ruth. The thought of the ten pounds he had more or less refused lay heavy on his conscience. "One shouldn't be sentimental about horses," he thought, staring at Trombone's familiar and beloved grey ears. But wasn't their effort to save the shire horses based on sentimentality? he asked himself. He cantered across a field, took the usual short cut to the Manse. "If only Trombone wasn't so promising, if she was just an ordinary horse, if only I didn't mean to show jump her next year," he thought. "Why did Ruth have to appear on the scene with her mass of dollars? Why did she have to pick on Trombone?"

"Here, put your hocks under you," he told the mare, driving her with his seat and legs. She came together, dropped her nose and relaxed her jaw, while underneath him she collected herself so that he thought, "Everybody's right – she has got prospects." For a second he felt elated; he saw Trombone competing in large competitions, her dressage improving, her jumping becoming bolder. Then he remembered Ruth, the way she looked at him, as though she knew that, in the end, she would win. "Perhaps she really can ride. After all, I'm no expert myself," he thought, reaching the Manse and riding round to the Victorian stable at the back. "The American teams are first class; they must have a mass of experts over there," he thought, dismounting. "She might even improve Trombone."

But he didn't believe that, couldn't imagine Ruth riding calmly, could only see her with waving arms and legs ... riding madly round the ring, while her fat and doting father watched from the ring ropes. He turned Trombone out and stood staring at the thistles. He decided where the ring would be and the position of the secretary's tent. Then he started to wonder about refreshments. Perhaps some caterers would come and pay for the privilege – his father would know. His parents were at church, the house was empty, except for the boxer, which welcomed him.

He found a billhook and a grass hook in the old glasshouse, which smelt of compost and stood shabby and unused by the back door. "What else shall we want this afternoon?" he wondered. "How big should a ring be? Where will Jocelyn's tent come from? Must I decide everything?

Surely the others will have some ideas," he thought wearily. For a moment he seemed to carry a ton on his shoulders. Then he shook himself. "I'm just being feeble," he thought. "Everything will work itself out. None of these beastly problems will alter the fate of nations."

After Nicholas had eaten a large helping of Sunday lunch, most of the gang arrived. First Ivor, panting, with a hot face, his hair plastered to his forehead.

"I came as quickly as I could. What shall I do?" he asked, as though there wasn't a moment to be lost.

"I was just going to start on the thistles."

"O.K." Replied Ivor picking up the grass hook. He was glad to be at the Manse. Sunday afternoon at home was no fun. His parents dozed in front of the television set and he had nothing in common with the boys loafing at the corner outside.

The Allcotts came next. Nicholas's heart sank when he saw that Ruth was with them.

"Hi. So this is where you live," she called. She had changed into a red shirt and a cleaner, newer pair of jeans.

"Ruth's come. I hope that's all right," said James apologetically.

"As long as she'll work," said Nicholas.

The Fishers arrived, carrying a tent.

"I don't know whether it's big enough. But we thought it might do for the Dog Gymkhana secretary at any rate," called Anne.

Maria was loaded with canvases.

"For the Dog Gymkhana wall," she said briefly.

Ivor was dressed in his Sunday clothes – white shirt, grey sweater, grey shorts and jacket, not to mention grey socks and black shoes. His hair was smothered with hair cream. He felt hot and uncomfortable. "Mum made me dress up," he told Maria, who wore a pair of red canvas shorts and a much-darned Aertex shirt. "She said I couldn't go to Captain Owen's place looking like a tramp."

"There's enough canvases here for two walls," Maria said.

"Doesn't your Dad want them any more?"

"I don't think so. They've been kicking about for ages."

Nicholas started to mark out the ring area with sticks. "I'm going to make it nearly three times as large as a dressage arena," he said.

"Let's look at the tent," Jocelyn suggested.

Gradually the gymkhana ground took shape. Bromwyn had brought materials with her and she started to work on the posters. Jocelyn and James put up the tent, while Ivor and Maria marked out the Dog Gymkhana ring.

Nicholas's confidence returned. "We're getting somewhere," he thought.

"I've done CAR PARK, LADIES, COLLECTING RING, SECRETARY'S TENT. What else do we need?" Bromwyn called.

"At least three saying TO THE SHOW," Nicholas answered.

Maria had made two walls. She stood back admiring them. "I'll find some brushwood for the brush fence now," she told Ivor.

Anne was going through the Manse's odds-and-ends box with Mrs. Owen. She kept saying, "Thank you, that will be lovely. Thank you," while the heap of old clothes at her side grew. At this moment, they were all optimistic; every minute they seemed to accomplish a bit more. None of them wondered what would happen after they had bought the three horses. "This time next Sunday it will all be over," thought James, "a weight will have been lifted from our backs. We will be able to relax."

Ruth stood talking to Trombone. "How about letting me try her?" she called to Nicholas. She was like a thorn in his flesh. "Haven't I got enough to worry about?" he thought.

"There isn't time," he called back.

"But I'm not doing anything."

"Have a go at the thistles then," shouted James.

But she didn't move, simply stood there, lanky and very American, talking to Trombone.

"When do her parents come out of hospital, James?" Nicholas asked.

"They're in a nursing home. They were staying in that new palatial hotel. I don't know, but she says they're nearly well again."

"Can she ride?"

"Yes. But I don't know how well." The two boys stood looking at Ruth. "She's riding tomorrow at Audrey's," James said.

"I must go now. Mum said I wasn't to be late for tea," Ivor announced. He had torn the back of his best shorts. "I'm borrowing plastic clothes lines for the ring ropes and I'll cut the stakes. The walls are lovely, Maria," he said. Tea would be laid; the kettle boiling; all the same he felt reluctant to go. "Do you think we'll make the two hundred pounds?" he asked James.

"I don't know. I just don't know."

"See you tomorrow at the riding school," Ivor said.

"We'd better all break up. I'll collect some posters from you in the morning, Bromwyn; otherwise I'm devoting the day to prizes," Nicholas said.

They gazed round the paddock. "I hope Trombone doesn't undo all our good work. If she tries, she'll have to sleep in the stable," Nicholas told the others. Ruth had joined them now. "You've sure done plenty," she said.

"Let's hope it's enough," James said.

"Two hundred pounds is such a little, just about six hundred dollars. It's not as much as our tickets over here," exclaimed Ruth. "What's your mare worth, Nick?"

"About two hundred at present, but if she keeps on improving she might be worth much more in a year's time. She jumps very well." Nicholas's throat felt dry. Trombone was the one thing which was really his; he hadn't another animal; his bicycle was old and bent. Trombone was his pride and joy. Mixed up with her were some of his dearest dreams and ambitions. "She and I are trying to improve ourselves together," he added, going across to the grey mare, putting his arms round her neck. "People say you only have one horse which really suits you in your life. The sort of horse which reads your thoughts, jumps over you when you fall before his feet and then waits for you to get on again. Well, she's that horse to me. I shall never have another horse like her. I feel it in my bones. That's why I'm selfish about her," he said. It was a very long speech for Nicholas. He wasn't accustomed to expressing so much; now suddenly he felt foolish. He turned away from the group and said in a completely different voice, "Well, let's clear up. Where's the grass hook?"

"What the heck is a grass hook?" asked Ruth.

In the Manse a gong was being banged. The day was cooling; the flies drifted away and in their place the midges came.

"Oh, for Virginia," thought Ruth. "For people who will lend you a horse and think nothing of it, for a Coca-Cola straight out of the icebox, for a great red sun sinking above the Blue Ridge Mountains." She had done nothing with her afternoon, she realised now. Nicholas didn't like her, never would like her or so it seemed. His mare was a heck of a mare, better than anything she had back home. She would like to buy her, to ship her to Virginia . . . But Nicholas was pig-headed – all the dollars in the world wouldn't buy his mare. Hadn't he said as much? She followed the other children, kicking a stone in front of her, and they, seeing a look of dislike on her face, looked the other way.

They called goodbye to one another and parted. The Fishers started to run. "I shall be up till midnight doing posters," Bromwyn exclaimed.

"I've got simply hundreds of things for my stall. It

must make at least fifty pounds. Someone will have to help me price them. Mrs. Owen is going to tell the Women's Institute about it on Wednesday," Anne shouted. (When the Fishers were together they always shouted).

"I made a smashing brush fence. Ivor wants me to be chief steward," Maria shouted.

"I wish we could ride in the gymkhana. Let's have a look at the shire horses before we go home," shouted Anne.

"I haven't time," yelled Bromwyn.

Ruth talked all the way home. She told the Allcotts about Virginia. How big her father's house was, how there was a coloured groom called Tommy; about the deep freeze and the hundred dollars' worth of steaks inside. About the herd of Red Polls and the way the sun went down in the evening; about the three cars – the convertible, the Cadillac and the new British Jaguar. She wanted to impress them, but James hardly listened and Jocelyn only replied "How smashing," or "How super!" at polite intervals.

The sun was going down now, but it wasn't a big red sun. Behind it were dirty slag heaps instead of distant mountains. Ruth felt suddenly homesick and had to bite her tongue to stop herself crying. Then she felt very angry. She wanted to insult the Allcotts; to hurt the pride she thought they had. Then she simply felt miserable. They came to the bungalow and tea was laid. James was doing sums in his head again; the three doomed horses were grazing. Jim Morgan was drinking beer, sitting on a stool in his ragged garden.

He waved to them and called, "Got the money yet?" and then began to laugh.

"How does he know we're in on it too?" James said.

"I don't know. How can he?" replied Jocelyn stupidly.

"He must have seen the posters. Don't they say IN AID OF UNWANTED HORSES?" reasoned James.

"Yes, that must be it."

They both looked gloomy now. Ruth had gone on ahead into the bungalow, where a telegram awaited her. "I feel something awful is about to happen," Jocelyn said, taking her spectacles off and wiping them. "I don't know why."

"Let's ignore him."

They found Ruth reading her telegram. "Daddy wants me to go and see him and Mummy tomorrow. He says I'm to hire a cab." She felt excited, much more cheerful. She would be able to tell her parents all about the riding school, about the gang, and, of course, about Nicholas. They might be coming out soon. They must be better. "Say, did you hear?"

"Yes," James said.

"How super. I bet you're pleased," Jocelyn cried, attempting enthusiasm.

"There's something horrible about him, something I can't describe. He gives me the creeps," said Jocelyn referring to Jim Morgan.

"Same here. I feel he's capable of anything," James agreed.

"Will you be able to get me a cab?" Ruth called to Mrs. Allcott, who was in the kitchen making the tea. "I'll want it after lunch."

"Jim Morgan's been round. He said he wanted the two hundred pounds by Saturday or not at all. He wasn't very pleasant. I don't know why you want to get mixed up with a man like him," Mrs. Allcott said, while James cried, "How can he? How can he be so unreasonable?"

"I knew something awful was going to happen," wailed Jocelyn.

"Can't you get it by Saturday?" asked Ruth.

"It'll be touch and go – a mass of pennies and small change. Just think of counting it out. The banks aren't open, you see," James replied. He could see a hundred difficulties now, they stretched ahead of him like a range of mountains, impossible to climb.

Mr. Allcott had come in from the garden. "I wish you

two kids wouldn't get mixed up with our neighbour. It's best to keep clear of a man like him," he said.

They could all see the horses grazing peacefully outside. "The grey is lovely," thought Jocelyn. "Why haven't we a farm? Why aren't we rich?"

"May I ring up Nicholas after tea, please?" asked James.

"Go ahead," his father answered.

"Well, I've finished already."

"But you haven't eaten anything," complained Mrs. Allcott.

"I'm not hungry. I'm sorry," he said, standing up.

"You mustn't be sentimental," his father answered. "Eat some bread and butter."

James sat down again. Dusk had come above the slag heaps; the sky was darkening. "There must be something we can do if we can't buy the horses," thought James. "Some loophole, a way out." He ate a piece of bread and butter, drank a cup of tea. His parents were talking to Ruth.

"Can I telephone now?" he asked, going into the front room. He knew Nicholas's number. His parents were still talking. "Will you be glad to be home again?" they asked Ruth.

"Yes, sure. America's a great country," she answered.

James was through now.

"Hullo, is that Captain Owen's house? Can I speak to Nicholas, please?"

His parents had stopped talking in the next room, but there was still the faint clink of cups, the scrape of knives against china.

Nicholas didn't have a high tea on Sunday evening like the Allcotts. The Owens had dinner in the evening, with table napkins, cut glass and three courses, starting with soup. Nicholas had been laying the table for his mother when the telephone rang. He was surprised to be called to the telephone, even more surprised to hear James's voice at the other end.

"But you've only just left," he objected.

"Bad news," announced James. "Jim Morgan's been here. He left a message. He wants the money by Saturday evening. It's his deadline."

There was silence while the words sank into Nicholas's brain. James's parents were talking again. Outside it was still dusk, the hot, dusty dusk of a hot August.

"How did he know you knew anything about it?" he asked Nicholas at last, while his brain digested this new surprise.

"I don't know. But things get around, don't they? Perhaps Ivor's father talked at the Men's Club, or Mr. Fisher. Does it matter?" asked James.

"We'd better see him right away. I'll be with you in fifteen minutes. What a beast he is," Nicholas said.

"But what are we to say?"

"I don't know yet. Do some thinking. I'll get out my bike. I don't know what the lights are like. Be seeing you."

"Be seeing you," James repeated, putting down the telephone receiver. He stood wondering how his parents would like this new visit to the Morgans. "Well, nothing venture, nothing win," he decided, returning to the small room which served both as play-room and dining-room.

His mother and Jocelyn were clearing away the plates.

"Finished?" asked his father, turning to the television set.

"Nicholas is coming. We're going to see Jim Morgan right away," James said.

Ruth's face lit up. "What here? You don't say . . ." she cried.

"It's a serious visit. A desperate visit. It won't be pleasant."

"I wish you wouldn't get mixed up with people like Morgan," his father repeated.

"I can go then?"

"If you must."

"What's happened? What did Nicholas say?" asked Jocelyn.

James started to explain. Somehow everything was beginning to seem rather futile. He felt that Jim Morgan was playing a cat-and-mouse game with them, that he was certain to win in the end, that all the dice were loaded against them.

Then there was a knock on the door and Nicholas stood outside, tall and determined in windcheater and jodhpurs.

"I've come without a light. I had to," he said. "Are you ready, James?"

"Hiya. Nice of you to stop by," called Ruth.

It was nearly dark, an owl was hooting and there was a pale moon hanging like a lantern in the indigo sky. The boys went out together. "Let's hope he's at home," James said.

"A lot of places are shut on Sunday night,"

"I know."

The brown gelding was lying down, large and cuddly, in the moonlight. The grey watched over him, while the bay gelding stood with his head over the gate and whinnied hopefully as the boys passed.

"We should have brought some sugar," James said.

"Have you any idea what we're going to say?" asked Nicholas.

"Not the faintest."

"Nor have I."

"We must trust to inspiration."

Nicholas liked James suddenly. He didn't like many people; he was more interested in doing things, rather than having close friends.

"There's a light on," James said.

"Mrs. Morgan won't be able to help. She's got no influence with him, poor woman."

The dogs were barking now and another light went on.

"Shall I speak first?" asked Nicholas.

"Yes, please."

The bay gelding was following them on the other side of a wire fence, his large, round muzzle stretched towards them.

"One can't help loving cart horses," James said. "I don't know why."

Nicholas opened the rickety garden gate. A crescendo of barking greeted them as they rapped on the sad, paint-chipped front door.

"Keep your fingers crossed," exclaimed Nicholas. And James obediently crossed his as the front door opened.

"Oh, it's you, is it?" Jim Morgan exclaimed. "You've soon come round. You got my message all right then?"

Nicholas assumed his father's voice.

"We certainly did. We're surprised that you've gone back on your word," he said.

"What do you mean?"

"You were going to give us ten days."

"Things have changed, see. I must have things settled by Saturday night one way or the other. If you can't find the cash they go on Monday. . . ."

"With the tide," James added.

"What do you know about tides?"

James thought a furrow creased Jim Morgan's narrow brow and was heartened. "There are plenty of cracks in his armour. We'll win yet," he muttered to Nicholas.

"It's your last word, is it? Saturday night or nothing? Let's get it quite clear, Mr. Morgan," Nicholas said.

"That's it, that's the way of it, that's the way I do business, see. I have to make a living. You can see we're not made of money here," said Jim Morgan.

"We'll be seeing you on Saturday night then, about eight I should think," Nicholas said. "And if we haven't the money, heaven help you, that's all I can say," Nicholas added, turning away in disgust.

"What I do is my own business. I don't want religion dragged into it," replied Jim Morgan, slamming the door.

"What a waste of time. I might as well have stayed at home," Nicholas said.

The bay gelding whinnied to them; again he walked alongside, his head over the wire.

"I'm glad Jim Morgan isn't our neighbour," Nicholas said.

The dogs were still barking. Somewhere a hen cackled.

"Maybe a fox is going to eat all his chickens," James said.

"It wouldn't teach him anything. He's simply out for what he can get and as crooked as a twisted nail. I won't come in. I'll go straight back. Can you lend me a torch or flashlight or anything for my bike?"

They were both dispirited. "It's all such a gamble," thought James. "Supposing it rains next Saturday? There won't be a hope of making two hundred pounds then."

"There's one in the garage," James said.

They fixed the light, before Nicholas rode away in the dark, his shoulders sagging disconsolately.

"Perhaps everything will look different in the morning," called James after the dry sound the tyres made on the unmade road.

He didn't want to go inside. Ruth would wish to know why Nicholas had gone so soon, as if he could explain. Jocelyn would want all the details of what had happened. In a way, the darkness suited James's mood. He could relax, listening to the wet sound of the shires grazing the dew-drenched grass. He could hear the bath taps running inside the bungalow; his father letting Tommy the cat out. A plane droned overhead and James wished suddenly that he was up there with the pilot far away from the beastliness of mankind. But he couldn't stay out all night. In a moment, his mother would open the door and call. Nicholas must be home by now. Was he relating to his parents everything that had happened? wondered James. Did they mind him visiting Jim Morgan?

"James, James, where are you?" called Mrs. Allcott.

The owl hooted as if in reply. All Jim Morgan's chickens were cackling now and the dogs had started to bark. James's moment of peace had gone.

"Coming," he called and went indoors.

More Bad News

Next morning they were all despondent. Ivor said a lot of words he wasn't allowed to use. Clutching a pile of schedules, Stella muttered, "Do you think the gymkhana will be in vain?"

"I suppose we'll just have to buy one of the horses, that's all," James announced.

The gloom had penetrated the stable yard. To make matters worse the day was cloudy, the forecast had promised rain, which made them all imagine a wet Saturday.

Steeped in army tradition, Nicholas tried to raise morale.

"However did you get the schedules done so quickly? You're marvellous, Stella," he said, and then, "For goodness' sake don't let's give up before we've even reached the battlefield."

Ruth was a maddening contrast to them all. She couldn't forget that she was visiting her parents after lunch. She felt as though she had been parted from them for a lifetime. How would they look? When would they be coming out? she wondered. Surely, by Saturday.

Nicholas had arrived after the rest of the gang, having been to Johnstown first. He had left Trombone at home simply because he wanted to keep his mare away from Ruth's admiring eye. It was maddening to have to ride his old bicycle the long way to the riding school, while Trombone grazed idly at home, simply because of a girl, an American girl at that.

The gloom prevailing in the stable yard depressed him further.

"What's the matter. You look as though you've all got the Monday morning blues," Audrey exclaimed cheerfully. "Come on, give a hand. Here, put Meadowsweet's saddle on, Jocelyn. Have all you turned to marble or something?"

"No, we've had bad news, that's all," James answered. But Audrey was too busy to hear or, if she did, the words didn't sink in. "You're riding Flashlight, Ruth," she called. "Come on, it's five to ten. Everyone get up."

There was the familiar sound of hoofs on gravel. Children mounted. "I feel like a wet rag this morning," Nicholas told James.

When the ride had gone, they started discussing prizes. They decided in the end that these would have to be taken from the entry money on the day and put in envelopes by the secretaries, Jocelyn and Stella; except, of course, for the prizes Nicholas had collected – his own cup, which was having its inscription and his name removed, a dandy brush from the saddlers and a pound from the corn merchants.

"I'm sure there's lots of things still to be settled," said Bromwyn. "What about refreshments?"

"I've fixed that up. We're being paid a percentage of the day's takings," Nicholas answered.

"I sent off twenty schedules last night," Stella said.

"And I did some telephoning. There should be a good Pony Club turnout," Nicholas told them.

"I haven't any Dog Gymkhana judges," Ivor announced. "Any suggestions?"

"Oh dear, let's think," said Anne.

"What about your father, Bromwyn?" asked Nicholas.

"No. He wouldn't accept, anyway."

"What about Mrs. Carson? She's on a mass of commitees, so she must be efficient," Anne suggested.

"And Mr. Jones. He's letting us use his yard as a car

park and he knows about dogs. I'll see him on the way home," offered Nicholas.

"And I'll see Mrs. Carson," said Anne. "She's sure to have lots of things for my stall."

"We had better make an alternative plan. What can we do to stop the horses going on Monday if we haven't all the money?" Bromwyn asked, while the others stared at her in amazement. "We must be like Machiavelli. Haven't you heard of him? Nicholas, you must have."

They remembered then that she had won a scholarship to the best girls' school in the district. Nicholas looked at her with more respect.

"That's a smashing idea," exclaimed Ivor. "Perhaps we can let the horses out."

"And be sued if there's an accident," answered Nicholas.

"It's best to keep on the right side of the law," stated James smugly.

"Is Jim Morgan on the right side of the law? Set a thief to catch a thief," quoted Bromwyn.

"Who can prove who opened the gate on Sunday night and drove the horses on to the waste land?"

"It would be better to stop the boat," Nicholas said.

"Yes, run down and say it isn't wanted after all," cried Bromwyn. "Wouldn't Jim Morgan be furious?"

"But we aren't sure about the boat, and we don't know where they're being shipped from," said James.

"Couldn't we waylay Jim Morgan, make him miss the boat?" asked Maria.

"Or cause a diversion," said Anne.

"If only we knew more about him," sighed Nicholas.

"We mustn't do anything criminal," James said.

It was raining now but their gloom had gone. There were new hopes on the horizon.

"We must study the tides. Obviously the horses will be loaded when the tide is in," Bromwyn said.

"But from where?" asked Nicholas.

"In secret. In the early morning; the boat comes in quietly . . . imagine it," Bromwyn cried.

"We might try to excite the horses so that they wouldn't load," suggested Stella.

"Yes," cried Ivor.

"Give them lots of oats," said James.

"And keep chasing them," added Jocelyn.

"That's an idea," agreed Nicholas. "Let's bear all these suggestions in mind and keep our eyes and ears wide open in the meantime. There must be some clues. We've still got a few days."

"And think and think and think," added Bromwyn.

Jocelyn and James were riding at eleven o'clock. Stella had brought her lunch as usual. Ivor had to return home. "Mum wants me to have a haircut and she's going to get me a new pair of shorts," he explained.

"If only we could be sure of something," thought James, restlessly watching the road for the ride's return. "If we only knew the weather would be fine on Saturday. If we knew we could raise the money or we couldn't. Nothing is definite. Even the length of Ruth's stay isn't certain." He paced up and down the road thinking: "Where is Jim Morgan going to take the three shire horses on Monday? What will we do if we don't raise the two hundred pounds?" Before he had answered these questions the ride came round the corner, Ruth leading, Audrey bringing up the rear on Periwinkle.

Nicholas hurried home to Trombone; then stood eating hunks of bread and cheese in the kitchen before he started to school her in the paddock. He rode mostly without stirrups; bumping up and down, driving the mare until his legs ached. His mind was in a turmoil. The battle against Jim Morgan had become very personal and Nicholas wasn't accustomed to losing battles. In addition, there was still the problem of Ruth and Trombone. He knew Ruth hadn't given up; she was still determined to ride his

mare on Saturday. He felt he was battling in all directions; that anything could still happen. Beyond these two battles stood his ambitions, his plans for Trombone.

"These holidays beat all the others for excitement," he decided ruefully, starting to ride. He wished now that he had never been drawn into trying to save the horses. He had seen nothing this holiday of his friends outside the gang; after Saturday he would have to make up for it. But Saturday still seemed an eternity away. "How I hate Jim Morgan," thought Nicholas.

The sky had cleared. The ground in the paddock was cracking beneath the short-cropped grass. "There's Tuesday, Wednesday, Thursday, Friday and then, at last, Saturday. A lot can happen in that time," decided Nicholas.

Ruth paid the taxi man and ran up the steps to Little Aden Nursing Home. "Why the heck Little Aden?" she wondered. "Isn't Aden in the desert somewhere?" She found a doorbell and pressed it.

"I've come to see my parents," she cried when a nurse came.

They had been given separate but adjoining rooms.

"Hi. Hiya. How are you doing?" Ruth cried.

She'd had the cabman stop on the way so that she could buy candy and flowers. Her mother was sitting in an armchair by her father's bed. Ruth gazed round the large room. "It's some place," she muttered.

After that she began to tell them everything which had happened. How small the Allcotts' house was, how they had high tea every evening; about the shire horses, about Nicholas and the riding school and Trombone.

"I should sure like that mare, Daddy," she finished. "And do you think you can give a prize for the gymkhana? Will you be out by then. Heck? I darn well hope so."

"Yes, should be. Here, give me my coat. Here's a twenty-dollar bill. How's that for a prize?" Mr. Barr was tall, broad-shouldered. "And we'll see what can be done about the mare," he added.

"I want to hire her for Saturday . . ."

"Go ahead. Pay what the boy asks."

"Oh, thank you, Daddy. But you'll be out of here by then?"

"Sure."

"Come and talk to me," her mother said.

She found another chair. "Nicholas is handsome, but real British, a real stuffed shirt," Ruth began.

Afterwards, travelling back to the Allcotts' bungalow in the taxi, which had waited outside Little Aden Nursing Home for an hour and a half, Ruth felt jubilant. Nicholas, she felt, would have to give in if she offered enough for the hire of Trombone on Saturday. The twenty-dollar prize would soften his stubbornness. She would sure have plenty to tell her friends when she got back home; perhaps Nicholas and she would correspond.

The Alcotts' house smelt of furniture polish when she reached it. Tea was on the table but she had had tea with her parents – thin slices of bread and butter, dry cakes, jam instead of the preserves they ate on bread back home.

The bungalow was gloomy. Somewhere, someone was crying. She found James standing in the small, cluttered kitchen, staring at the cooker. He seemed to be in a dream; for James, he was untidy – one shoelace was undone, his hair was on end, and he hadn't washed his hands.

"Say, what's happened?" cried Ruth.

"Jim Morgan's moved the horses. We don't know where. Can't you see what that means?" James said.

"But you can still buy them."

"If we raise two hundred pounds. But it may rain. How do we know people are going to turn up? Perhaps he's shipped the horses already. He's capable of anything. All this work for nothing – all the worry. We can't even ride in the gymkhana," James cried.

"Have you told Nicholas?"

"Not yet."

"Shall I call him up?"

"No, please no."

"Don't get mad at me."

"I'm not."

"Oh, you crazy Britishers! And I've just got a prize for you in my purse. Look, a twenty-dollar bill," cried Ruth, holding it under James's nose.

"I'm sick of thinking about money. But thanks all the same," he replied, taking it.

"But I was going to give it to Nicholas."

"But I'm treasurer. Sorry, how are your parents? I should have asked."

"They'll be at the gymkhana on Saturday. It *was* food poisoning. They're okay now."

"I must make the tea. Jocelyn, tea! Mummy, tea!" James called. He felt as limp as a damp dishcloth. It had been awful to come home and find the field empty. He and Jocelyn had simply stood and stared, their mouths open. All their dreams and hopes had toppled. The little certainty there had been had gone. Jim Morgan was sitting outside his door, cleaning a gun. Mrs. Morgan was working in the garden as usual. The field gate was shut.

"Shall we go and speak to him?" James had asked. Without waiting for his sister's reply, he had started to run towards Jim Morgan's bungalow.

"Shouldn't we consult the others?" Jocelyn cried, following. The whole place was shabby beneath the sun.

"Good afternoon to you," Jim Morgan had cried and James had seen a leer on his face and had regretted his hasty decision to ask after the horses.

"Are you looking for something?" Jim Morgan asked.

"You haven't sold the horses, have you?" James asked, and all the anxiety he felt was in his voice.

"Sold them? They've been sold for a long time," Jim Morgan laughed. "But you're still open to buy them for two hundred. I'll keep to my word – two hundred."

James glanced at the stable. It was a ramshackle building, but the doors were open. "You won't find them here," Jim Morgan said, his eyes following James. "I've sent them somewhere convenient for Monday."

It was when they left that Jocelyn had started to cry. "I just can't help it. I'm sorry," she kept saying, while the tears flooded her cheeks.

"Now what's the matter?" cried Mrs. Allcott when she saw them. "Who has been upsetting you now?"

"He's moved them," cried Jocelyn. "How will we ever save them now? How will we, Mummy? We don't even know where they are. I've got so fond of them. They're so much nicer than people," she said.

"You've been overdoing it, worrying. Look at the time you've been getting up each morning. You're tired, that's all. Everything will seem different in the morning. Let's get tea, shall we?" Mrs. Allcott put her arm round Jocelyn. "We'll think of something," she promised.

But they hadn't thought of anything by the time Ruth returned. Jocelyn couldn't stop crying. It was as though a dam had burst. "And I'm eleven," she kept thinking, "I'm sure Ruth never cries."

Ruth was full of her afternoon.

Jocelyn went straight to bed after tea. Although she knew the horses had been sent away, her eyes kept straying to the field, half hoping to see their familiar figures again. Ruth and James watched television. James couldn't concentrate. He felt he had let the gang down by calling on Jim Morgan. What would Nicholas say when he heard everything in the morning? Shouldn't James have pretended indifference? As it was, he had played into Jim Morgan's hand. He felt a fool.

When he went to bed he couldn't sleep for hours. He wakened late. Jocelyn was still sleeping, but Ruth was in the kitchen telling Mrs. Allcott about Virginian breakfasts.

"We have waffles and bacon with maple syrup. Have you ever eaten waffles, Mrs. Allcott?" she asked. James hated her at that moment, hated everything. His head

ached, his legs felt like lead, his heart as heavy as the weights in a corn merchant's shop.

"Breakfast is nearly ready. Jocelyn is still asleep, so don't make a noise," his mother said. He went outside and there was the empty field staring at him, and, for some reason, it seemed his fault that there were no horses there grazing beneath the morning sun. The sky was quite clear. He knew at once that the day was to be stifling. Standing there, he swore to himself that today, at least, he'd have a swim. When had he last swum? Not for a week at least – years ago it seemed, so old did he feel now.

His mother sensed his despair as he went in to breakfast.

"Cheer up, dear, things pass," she said. "Life is long and time is a great healer."

"I feel at least a hundred," James replied.

Ruth was still describing Virginian breakfasts. Already it was hot in the small room. James disappeared upstairs in search of his bathing trunks.

Coming down again, preparing to leave, he said, "Do you want to come to the riding school now, Ruth?" He would rather have gone alone, but she cried, "Sure, hold on a minute."

A moment later they were walking together through the hot sunlight.

"It's a funny thing to say, but I sure miss those three farm horses. I guess I'd just got used to seeing them out there," Ruth said.

Jim Morgan was sitting in the sun, this time with the morning paper in his hand. "Doesn't he ever do an honest job of work?" wondered James. A sea breeze fanned their faces as they neared the riding school. Flies were everywhere; children already playing on the beach below.

"It's sure cute around here. Look at that cute cottage," cried Ruth.

James could see the Fisher girls approaching the riding school from the other direction. He had to stop to remember which day it was – Tuesday! How many days did that leave them? Really only three more.

Ruth had put on her best jeans. "Will Nicholas be there?" she asked.

"I expect so," James said.

They had reached the riding school now. The sun shone hot on the corrugated roofs. Some of the ponies were sweating already. "There won't be much serious riding today," thought James.

"Say, there's Trombone," cried Ruth as she entered the yard. "Nick must be somewhere around then."

What Have You Done Now?

Nicholas felt better. He had spent the evening before telephoning his other friends, explaining why he hadn't seen them for so long. To his surprise, they had all promised to come to the gymkhana and three of them had offered silver cups they had won for running or tennis. "You mean as prizes?" Nicholas had asked each time. They had replied, "Of course, what do you think, dope?" Or, "No, to cook in."

He had invited them all to a swimming party on the Wednesday after the gymkhana. Only later, when he was in bed, did he start to wonder what they would do if it was wet.

Waking in the morning, lying in bed while gulls screeched overhead and a hot sun played on his counterpane, he decided to be firm with Ruth. If she asked to ride Trombone, he would say simply but firmly, "For the first and last time the answer is '*No*'." She couldn't argue with that, even an American couldn't, he decided.

When he got up he saw that Trombone was already under the trees, switching her grey tail against the flies. He whistled as he dressed and thought about the swimming party and how wonderful life would be when Saturday

was over, the horses bought and Ruth once more with her parents. He sang loudly as he brushed his fair hair. Running downstairs, he counted up the prizes he had collected. "Six," he thought, "that'll save us about five pounds." His parents were still in bed, so he made them tea and took it upstairs. The garden was full of sunlight, and he could just see the sea from their bedroom window, lapping gently against the sand. A few early risers were walking their dogs along the beach. A boy threw stones at the waves. Life suddenly seemed peaceful. "Surely, if we don't raise two hundred pounds on Saturday we can still fox Jim Morgan somehow or other," thought Nicholas.

"Off to the riding school? You almost live there," his mother said.

"Yes. But after Saturday I shall be at home more," answered Nicholas, leaving the room.

There were three letters in the post for him and all contained entries for the gymkhana and the appropriate entry fees. "They should have been sent to the Allcotts' really," thought Nicholas, stuffing them into his jodhpurs pockets. The daily woman had arrived and was cooking breakfast.

"What's all this about you buying Jim Morgan's horses? It's all over the village," she said.

"It's quite true," replied Nicholas, helping himself to fishcakes and eating them off the corner of the kitchen table. At that moment, it seemed perfectly possible, anything seemed possible.

Trombone welcomed him with a whinny, pushed her nose into her bridle and seemed impatient to be on the road and on her way to the riding school.

Nicholas called goodbye to his parents before he left.

Trotting across the small, sloping fields which took him the quickest way to the riding school, his mind considered Saturday. There didn't seem much left to do – the judges were settled, the jumps, car park, refreshments, prizes, ring ropes, petty cash and at least one tent. The only things which couldn't be settled were the weather and the number of people likely to be present. With the sun shining, Nicholas felt optimistic on both these scores – the weather would bring the people and the weather didn't look like changing. "Why on earth was I so gloomy yesterday?" wondered Nicholas, getting off to open a difficult gate. Now he could see the riding school and Audrey going from loose box to loose box with a wheelbarrow.

"Good old Audrey," thought Nicholas. "What would we all do without her? At least you can depend on her to be the same wet or fine."

Ivor had cut the stakes for the Dog Gymkhana ring; he had arranged to borrow eight plastic clothes lines; with the last of his savings he had bought a thick ball of string to rope off the collecting ring. Five of his friends had promised to bring their dogs. Running the sea way to the riding school, he felt as bright as the morning. "We're going to succeed," he thought, "I feel it in my bones." His pockets bulged with thick cheese sandwiches made by his mother. "I must give old Pete a jumping lesson this evening," he decided. He met Stella getting off the bus carrying a paper bag, which she opened to reveal rosettes.

"Will these do?" she asked.

"Smashing. Tophole," Ivor replied.

"The Dog Gymkhana's going like clockwork," he thought. "But when we get the horses, what are we to do with them?" He hadn't thought of that before. Would Nicholas keep them in his paddock? But for how long? "They'll need a home," he decided, and imagined them working on a farm, ploughing as a team beneath an evening sky, with the slag heaps in the background and the sea below. "That's it, we'll give them to a farm," he said out loud.

"Give what?" asked Stella. Neat and clean, she was dressed in riding clothes for, as she had said earlier to her mother, "You never know who will fail to turn up. I'm sure it's my turn for the next free ride."

"The horses to a farm."

"But we haven't bought them yet."

"But we're going to, even if we can't buy them right away, we'll save them some way or other. I feel it in my bones."

"Only because the sun's shining. If it was raining, everything would appear quite different."

"Look, there are the Fishers," Ivor cried. "I've got to ask Nicholas for a loan of a pound to buy the prizes. I'm only going to give things like rubber bones, and balls and dog biscuits."

"And brushes and combs for the dogs," Stella added.

They had reached the riding school now and could see Nicholas tying up Trombone. Sunshine was everywhere. Dust was rising as Audrey swept the yard.

"Phew! It's going to be hot," exclaimed Ivor.

"You're telling me," agreed Stella.

The Fisher girls had got their own breakfast. Not that they bothered much over the meal, though their mother insisted that they ate something cooked on school mornings.

"I wonder whether there have been any entries yet," Bromwyn said, as they hurried along the road.

"I don't know how I'm to carry all my things to the Manse on Saturday if it's raining," Anne remarked.

"It's not going to rain," shouted Bromwyn. "Look at the sky. We're in for a heat wave."

"Then there's Daddy's pictures. I wish I hadn't got to try and sell them. Whoever will want to buy an oil painting of a slag heap for five guineas. Five shillings would be different but five guineas!" exclaimed Anne.

"Don't be beastly about Daddy," shouted Maria.

"I'm not."

"You are."

"For goodness' sake don't start quarrelling. Look, there

are James and Ruth. I wonder what has happened to Jocelyn," said Bromwyn, in the conciliatory tones of an elder sister.

"I think Ruth's awfully pretty," Anne said.

They waved to James and Ruth. "Where's Jocelyn?" called Bromwyn.

"Still asleep."

"James sounds gloomy," Anne said.

Bromwyn and Anne waited for James and Ruth.

"I hope there are some entries," Bromwyn said.

The four children went into the yard together, Ruth towering above the other three.

"I've got some bad news," James said in a flat voice devoid of emotion. "I think we'd better meet in the granary."

"Oh no," cried Bromwyn. "What is it this time?"

Ruth and James approached Nicholas together.

"Hiya, so you've brought Trombone again," Ruth said.

"Bad news," James announced. "Do you think we can all meet in the granary?"

"Is it that important?" asked Nicholas, his previous mood of optimism fading to be replaced by a sense of annoyance.

"What have you done now?" he demanded, suddenly angry, while he saw a host of difficulties ahead, where five minutes ago all had seemed smooth and simple.

"What have I done now? I like that," retorted James.

"I want to talk with you, Nick," Ruth said.

The boys faced one another angrily, ignoring the girl completely, before James's anger drained away and he was left feeling that everything was his fault.

"After all it was Jo's and my idea in the beginning," he said.

"Sometimes I wish you had never set eyes on the horses," Nicholas replied.

It was very hot now and the corrugated roofs seemed

to throw the heat back at them. There wasn't the faintest breeze, not a cloud in the sky, only the promise of a heat wave.

"All right, let's meet in the granary; perhaps it's cooler there," Nicholas said.

"Nick, I want to talk with you. Nick," it was Ruth tugging at his arm, a thorn in his flesh again. What had he meant to say to her? He couldn't remember now. Perhaps he should let her hire Trombone. Wouldn't it mean ten dollars? Ten dollars! But not a fortune. "Later, I'm busy now." She let go of his arm and he felt suddenly sorry for his abruptness. On an impulse he said, "I'm having a swimming party Wednesday week, will you come?" She was ridiculously pleased and, of course, he was flattered.

Following James to the granary, he thought, "She's got her good points, she's ready to fight for what she wants. Perhaps I'll let her have Trombone."

The others were there already.

"The horses have disappeared," announced James.

"You mean he's sold them?" cried Ivor.

"No, he's moved them to somewhere more convenient. You see, I went to see him when I saw they had gone. Jocelyn came too. I think he expected us." It was said now; James wondered why he had worried so much. What he had done wasn't criminal.

"What did he say exactly?" Nicholas asked.

James tried to remember. "He asked if we were looking for something. There was a nasty twinkle in his eye. He said we were still able to buy them for two hundred. Then he told us that they had been put somewhere more convenient for Monday," James related.

"They're not sold. That's the main thing. I thought your ill tidings were going to be much worse," Nicholas said.

"They're bad enough. How can we put our second plan into action if we don't know where the horses are?" Bromwyn asked.

"We must find them," Ivor said. "We've got legs and Nicholas has a horse."

"But they may be fifty miles away," objected Nicholas.

"I don't think so. Mummy would have seen the horse-box or cattle truck, even if we didn't. I think he's moved them nearer the sea," James said.

"If we do get the two hundred, we'd better get a receipt from Jim Morgan before we hand over all the money," Nicholas suggested.

"You really do think he's a crook?"

"Yes."

"We'll all keep an eye out for the horses then; make inquiries. Daddy may see them. He gets about a good deal," Bromwyn said, getting up from the bale of hay on which she had been sitting. "Can I come over to your place this afternoon, Nicholas? I've managed to borrow a super tent. I want to get it up in plenty of time. Then I can bring the table and chair along, and Jocelyn can use it as an office."

"Yes, all right. I don't suppose Trombone will knock it down," replied Nicholas.

They left the granary and started to help Audrey. Ruth was waiting for Nicholas.

"Have you decided anything? Daddy will pay anything you ask, just ask," she said.

"You'd better try her first," Nicholas didn't feel like fighting any more. "Perhaps he would like to give a contribution towards the horses. You can have Trombone for nothing, if you can manage her."

"You mean it? Say, that's real nice of you."

"Come this evening and we'll see how you get on," he said. It was a relief to have said, "Yes," to have given in. At least his conscience was clear. Mr. Barr might give ten pounds, five, at any rate, "If only Ruth doesn't ruin Trombone's jumping," he thought.

All the ponies were sweating now. "Audrey won't let anyone do much this morning," thought Nicholas. "Really riding in this weather is a dead loss."

"What classes can I ride her in?" asked Ruth.

"We'll decide this evening. I can't think now."

Nicholas decided to go home, from there he would make inquiries as to the whereabouts of the shire horses. Later he might swim. Visitors were appearing to ride, dressed in the strangest clothes; one girl in a bathing dress, another in a flowered frock. Nicholas was glad to leave, to ride homewards through the hot morning, imagining a drink out of the refrigerator.

"There's plenty of time till Saturday," he kept telling himself. "We don't have to work ourselves to death before Friday."

Meanwhile, Ruth was boasting of her triumph.

"I'm riding Nick's horse tonight. I guess he doesn't hate me after all. I'm riding her on Saturday, too."

The members of the gang were surprised. Suddenly the lustrous Nicholas lost a little of his glitter. Ivor was angry.

"You bullied him into it," he cried angrily.

The yard seemed suddenly full of anger. Jocelyn, entering at that moment, sensed the feeling. "We're beginning to hate one another," she thought. "We don't get on any more." A fly landed in her eye and she stood still, holding her spectacles and trying to get it out with the corner of her handkerchief.

"Have you heard, Jo? I'm riding Trombone tonight," Ruth called.

"I suppose she's responsible. Why did she come to stay? Why did she pick on our place?" wondered Jocelyn.

James passed her, his bathing trunks in his hand. "Going swimming. You must look after Ruth now. I've done my share for today," he muttered.

"He hasn't, but that's boys all over," decided Jocelyn. "They'll never stick at anything for more than ten minutes."

"Nicholas left these entries for you. There's some money here too," called Stella.

"And I've got another tent," shouted Bromwyn.

The Cove

The long beach below the riding school was crowded with people. They seemed to cover every inch of it.

James decided to go further along the coast. He knew a cove which could be approached only by a path across fields, followed by a treacherous descent. He finished his ice and started to run. A sea breeze fanned his face; the air was salt; overhead, gulls wheeled.

He left the beach by a winding path which led between sand dunes. The sand was fine and white; the sun so bright that it hurt his eyes. He was glad to reach the small golf course above, to turn left, to cross the railway line, ignoring the warning of a fine for trespass and to reach a parched field cracked by drought. It was very quiet here after the beach, though he could hear the occasional sound of golf club against ball.

He climbed through a wire fence and now he could see the sea again, as gentle as a lake beneath the hot sun. He started to run again. He judged the time to be eleven o'clock and he hadn't reached the cove yet. "I'll be late for lunch," he kept thinking, "and Mummy hates that." Sweat was running down his face now. He longed for the sea, as much as one does for a large meal when one is famished.

He thought, "I don't care. Nothing will make me turn back now." He was a long way from the road. Some sheep stood panting under a tree. He seemed the only other moving thing for a brief moment. Then he ducked under a fence, stopped short in his tracks and stood staring. Suddenly his flagging spirits soared and the swim didn't matter any more, only the three large horses which stood head to tail under a solitary tree.

"I've beaten Jim Morgan after all," he thought, "no

one can grumble at me now." He went up to the horses and patted their necks under their long tangled manes. They turned their simple, roughly-carved heads and looked at him with gentle eyes and nuzzled him with soft noses. They were covered with flies and the grey had a festering wound on one fetlock. James saw, for the first time, old collar sores on the bay's neck. He couldn't help thinking that their characters compared favourably with Jim Morgan's, for there was nothing sly about them.

He left them and started the treacherous descent to the beach. The cove was quite empty. The deserted sand seemed to be calling him down to swim. He was suddenly happier than he had been in his whole life.

Then something else caught his eye, a gate and a path he had never noticed before. In a flash, he realised everything – this was where the boat would come from Ireland on Monday; it would be an illegal boat. Why else should it come to a deserted cove? In one corner of the cove the sea was deep, deep enough to bring in a fair-sized boat. There was also a flat rock from which quiet horses could be loaded.

James changed behind a rock and plunged into the sea. Lying on his back, staring at the sky, he felt at peace. "At least I've found them," he thought. Presently he realised how late it must be; the sun had moved considerably in the sky, the sea was going out. He swam briskly to the shore, dressed quickly and looked in all directions before he started to climb to the horses' field.

Feeling triumphant, he started to run. The swim had given him new energy. He felt that he could run for ever, that nothing would ever daunt him again, least of all Nicholas or Jim Morgan. The golf course was empty which meant it was lunch time or later. James was very hot now; his wet bathing trunks and damp towel seemed to weigh pounds and his legs ached. He reached the road. He was sure no-one had seen him, not even when he trespassed on the railway line. He started to walk then, for he was nearly

The three large horses stood head to tail under a solitary tree

home. He could hear cries coming from the beach. The road was crowded with cars and, somewhere, a wireless blared hot music into the hot afternoon. Walking that last piece home, James felt he had achieved more than the rest of the gang put together. He started to whistle. He had reached the bungalow and his mother standing on the front doorstep, calling, "Oh, James, I thought you were never coming, that something had happened. What have you been doing? It's past two o'clock."

He felt remorseful then, for, even if he washed up, his mother wouldn't get her sit-down now. But his sense of triumph didn't diminish. He called, "I've found the horses," – before he saw that Jim Morgan was sitting by his shack reading the paper.

Nicholas had hoped that Bromwyn would leave before Ruth arrived. But she continued obstinately cutting down thistles, long-legged, disreputable in paint-stained shorts, dirty white plimsolls and faded Aertex shirt. Nicholas had tired of work more than an hour ago. The tent was up with the notice SECRETARY'S TENT displayed outside. The sun was going down, people were leaving the beach; another day was ending. Nicholas had saddled and bridled Trombone. He felt apprehensive. What words could he use to tell Ruth that she couldn't ride well enough?

She arrived at last, breathless, calling, "Hi, Nick. Do you know what? James has found the horses. I'm on my way back from the nursing home."

"Found the horses?" repeated Nicholas.

"Yeah, by some cove or other." She stood patting Trombone now. "Thanks for tacking up your mare," she added.

"Which cove?"

"A secret one, he said."

Bromwyn had joined them now. "Hurray, good old James," she exclaimed. "That gives us a chance to put a second plan into action."

"You'd better get up, Ruth. Perhaps we won't need a second plan," Nicholas replied, piqued because James had found the horses instead of himself.

"I'll push off. Have a nice ride, Ruth," Bromwyn said.

Nicholas pulled up the grey mare's girths. "You'd better just walk at first, see how you get on."

"Sure."

The girl fitted Trombone; she rode with long reins and a loose seat. "She sure walks like a show horse," she exclaimed.

"She's had a lot of schooling," Nicholas said. "Try collecting her a little, shortening the reins; now what about a trot?"

Seeing Ruth on Trombone wasn't hurting as much as he had expected. True she rode without much contact but that was better than riding with too much. Ruth trotted and he thought, "Perhaps it'll be all right." His spirits started to rise. Presently Ruth was cantering, calling out, "She's swell, Nick, great. Sure you won't part with her?"

"Sure." Nicholas shouted back. He was suddenly glad that Ruth was riding Trombone. "Perhaps they'll win something on Saturday and that will be another rosette to pin on my bedroom wall," he thought. "Oh, she's great, Nick," Ruth called again. He liked her for her enthusiasm.

"How about a jump now?" Nicholas asked.

She drew rein and patted Trombone. "She must be a great hunter," she said.

"She is."

Nicholas found some poles and supports. He put up parallel bars two feet high and three feet apart. "Can you jump that?"

"Sure."

Ruth rode very fast and, with a sudden spurt, Trombone galloped past the jump.

"Let's have a talk," Nicholas suggested.

"I know it's darned well my fault. I'm sorry, Nick."

"You'd better just walk at first"

"It's just that we ride differently. Your horses probably wouldn't understand my aids," Nicholas said. He didn't want to hurt the girl, he wanted her to like him, to go back home remembering him.

"We don't jump flat out, not unless we're racing," began Nicholas and they both knew suddenly that this was the beginning of a friendship. Nicholas lectured and Ruth listened. Then she tried the mare again. "How's that?" she called as they cleared the fence.

"Quite different. Let's pull your stirrups up a hole then it will be better still; you're still a little far back in the saddle. What do you want to enter for on Saturday?"

"Everything I can, Nick."

The gong was sounding now for the evening meal.

"You'd better stay to dinner. We can ring up the Allcotts. I'll see you home. And you can come again tomorrow for another lesson."

They turned Trombone out together. The sun was setting, a mist was rising above the sea. "I wish Saturday was here. It seems to have been hanging over us for an age. We'd better go in," Nicholas said.

The meal was on the table. "Can Ruth stay to dinner" Nicholas asked.

He fetched another plate, more cutlery.

"James has found the horses. They're near a cove. Things are beginning to move," he said.

"What part of America do you come from, Ruth?" asked Captain Owen.

There was soup and shepherd's pie, sardines on toast and cheese. When they had finished dusk had come.

"Let's go," Ruth said.

The air smelt of soot, of myrtle and thyme, of the sea and seaweed. "I rang up James. He's afraid Jim Morgan heard him mention the horses. Poor James, he always puts his foot in it somehow or other," Nicholas said.

"Jocelyn was crying last night."

"Whatever for?"

"Because the darned horses had gone."

Cars full of noisy travellers passed them. On the far hill the lights were on in the hundred caravans parked on the Hilltop Site.

"You'll come and ride again tomorrow then?" Nicholas asked.

"You bet."

"I want to give everyone a surprise. They all think you can't ride much."

They had reached the bungalow now. Outside, James stood waiting for them.

"No more news. Nothing's happened since you telephoned," he called, as though living in a permanent state of emergency.

"Did you expect the house to get burnt down or something?" asked Nicholas.

"It's all very well to laugh. Jo and I are getting quite jittery about Jim Morgan. It's all right for you, he's not your neighbour."

"What do you think he's likely to do?"

"I don't know."

"You'd better buy a revolver."

"Funny, funny."

"I'm glad you found the horses anyway. Where exactly are they?" asked Nicholas.

"I don't suppose you know the place. You have to cross the railway line where it's illegal." Quite suddenly James ceased to admire Nicholas. He felt his equal now. Behind them, Jocelyn opened a window. "Mummy says Ruth should be in bed," she whispered.

"Oh, heck," Ruth said.

"I'd better be getting back. It's nearly dark. I don't want Jim Morgan to get me," said Nicholas with a laugh.

"I'll be right over after breakfast," Ruth answered.

"Fine. Before it's hot."

"My, the field looks empty without the horses."

They stood there a moment longer and saw that Jim Morgan's lights were going out one by one.

"See you tomorrow then," called Nicholas, walking away down the road, his hands in his pockets and his mind on Ruth.

"Do you want any more to eat, Ruth?" asked James.

"Heck, no."

The television was on. Moths fluttered on the outside of the windows. "I think Nick's great. I'm turning in. Good night, James," Ruth said.

"Today is over but tomorrow there will be another day with a lot more opportunities," thought James. "I never thought Nicholas would fall for Ruth. How extraordinary life is." He was very tired now.

"Good night all," he called, going upstairs, entering his bedroom and starting to undress.

The Day Before

Wednesday and Thursday passed without incident. Nicholas gave Ruth a riding lesson on Trombone on each of these days. On Friday morning, her parents came out of the nursing home and drove in a pale blue and chromium coupé to the Allcotts' bungalow.

They were different from what anyone expected. There was nothing loud-voiced or brash about them. They brought presents for Jocelyn and James – a huge box of candy and a sheath knife which James stuck immediately in his belt. They brought Mrs. Allcott flowers – a great bunch of hot-house carnations which seemed too opulent for the sitting-room. They were immensely grateful.

"We sure don't know what we would have done without your help, Mrs. Allcott," they kept saying.

"I've had a wonderful time," added Ruth, thinking of the rides she had enjoyed on Trombone.

"She'll never forget it," promised Mrs. Barr.

Jocelyn helped Ruth pack her hold-all.

"They want me to go back to the hotel with them. But I'm still riding on Saturday. When I get home, I'll write you," the American girl said.

"That'll be lovely," replied Jocelyn politely.

"Now we're going to Nick's place," Ruth said, rejoining her parents, hold-all in hand.

The bungalow seemed very quiet when they had gone. Jocelyn started writing out the entries she had received, giving each one a number. The heatwave hadn't abated; she wore only sandals and a spotted sun-suit. The wireless was on; she could smell the rice pudding cooking in the oven. She realised suddenly how dull the bungalow seemed without Ruth.

"We ought to have cadged a lift. I'm off to the Manse now," James said. "This is the last day, do you realise that? Tomorrow will decide." He went out, slamming the front door behind him. He was pent up, with notes of things to remember in his pocket and the hot sun in his eyes. Mrs. Morgan was digging in the garden. The dogs sprawled around the doorstep. "Another scorcher," thought James. "I hope it rains on Sunday, the ground's like concrete."

Ruth had gone when he reached the Manse. "Hallo," called Nicholas.

The Dog Gymkhana ring was up and the tents were in place; the jumps were neatly stacked by the gate. Anne was putting up a trestle table. Ivor stood hammering a wooden stake into the dry earth. "The ground's like reinforced concrete," he called.

"Some peat's coming after lunch. Audrey said her ponies couldn't jump otherwise. It's an awful expense," grumbled Nicholas.

Stella was in the Dog Gymkhana tent, labelling rosettes. The whole field was like a beehive in action.

"I'm afraid I'm late. Ruth's parents came," James explained.

"They're nice, aren't they?" asked Nicholas, handing James a sledgehammer.

The boys took off their shirts. The heat was almost unbearable; from time to time thunder rumbled in the distance.

Presently, Jocelyn arrived with a pile of papers in a shoe-box and disappeared into the larger of the two tents marked SECRETARY. She was nervous now. Supposing she had forgotten something vital. Luckily, her father had once helped run a horse show and had given her copious advice. She started to sort through the numbers Bromwyn had made. They went up to eighty. They were to be worn on the rider's arms, on their left arms, decided Jocelyn.

Ivor and Maria began whitewashing the Dog Gymkhana jumps. Suddenly someone cried, "What about the music? We must have music for the musical poles!"

"You mean we haven't done anything about it?" cried Bromwyn. "Oh dear, how awful."

"We can always blow a whistle. They do sometimes at shows," said James.

"I've got a record-player and a radio pick-up," Nicholas said.

"Perhaps we could run it off a car."

"Leave it to me, anyway," Nicholas said.

He was thinking about Ruth. Her father had pressed a fifty-dollar bill into his hand. "Don't thank me, son; it's for the horses you're saving," he had said. Fifty dollars! He hadn't mentioned it to the gang yet. He couldn't help sensing that they disapproved of Ruth riding Trombone, but then they didn't know how much she had improved. He had decided to tell them about the money afterwards, when they realised that he wasn't such a fool after all. Fifty dollars – about fifteen pounds he reckoned.

The main ring was up at last. Nicholas and James started to erect the collecting ring. The paddock echoed with the sound of hammers. Today no one chattered – there was too much still to be done, too much to worry about. At lunchtime they went their separate ways. There was still thunder in the air, which gave everyone the feeling that anything might happen or, as Stella said simply, "the woollies". She had what her mother called the "needle", a funny feeling in her tummy. Her mother had promised to help if she became muddled. Stella had burst into tears on Thursday evening, quite suddenly, "I know I shan't be able to do it. I don't know how to be secretary and Nicholas and Ivor will be furious if I make a muck of it." She had cried.

Her mother had consoled her; they had gone backwards and forwards through the arrangements together, until now Stella knew it all by heart, rather as an actor knows his lines before going on the stage. But that didn't stop her feeling nervous. She went back to the riding school and ate her sandwiches in the saddle-room. The thunder rumbled and her needle became worse every moment.

The Allcotts returned home for lunch. There was no sign of Jim Morgan nor of his wife; James found he looked for them every time he passed the field where the horses had been.

And now, suddenly, quite unreasonably, he felt he must see the horses, find out if they were in the same field before Saturday dawned. He felt their presence or absence would be a vital piece of information, of immense importance. "I'll go tonight," he told himself.

Neither he nor Jocelyn ate much lunch for they were impatient to be back at the Manse working in the paddock.

The whole gang worked for the rest of the day; by five o'clock the paddock really did look like a show ground.

"I'll put the rest of the signs up later," Bromwyn said.

Nicholas was impatient to be rid of the gang. Ruth was to have her final lesson at six-thirty, while her parents drank sherry with Captain and Mrs. Owen. He wanted to keep it secret, to let Ruth's riding surprise the whole gang the next day.

"That's all done then until six-thirty a.m.," he said.

There was still thunder in the air, so that James kept thinking, "If only the storm would break!"

"Doesn't the Dog Gymkhana ring look smashing?" asked Ivor. He couldn't believe now that he was running the Dog Gymkhana, that because of him the ring was there; he kept expecting something to go wrong.

"I'll bring some cakes for your stall tomorrow," Stella announced.

"You're an angel," Anne replied. Everything was priced now and stacked in the greenhouse, covered by a dust sheet. Only her father's paintings remained to be brought in the morning.

"Well, I must be getting along. Tea must be nearly ready," Ivor told the others. "I expect Mum will buy some things from your stall, Anne; she loves a good rummage sale," he added.

"We'd better go too," James told Jocelyn. "We've still got things to do at home. At least I have," he said and thought of his secret visit to the horses. Thunder was still rumbling. The sky had grown darker.

"I'd better leave my signs until tomorrow if it's going to rain," Bromwyn said.

"Goodbye, everyone. I'll come on the first bus in the morning," Stella cried, walking away across the paddock with her school satchel swinging on her back.

Only the Fishers lingered now and it was nearly six o'clock. "Surely it's your tea-time," Nicholas suggested.

"Nobody bothers about meal-times in our house," Maria answered.

"There must be something else which needs doing, isn't there?" Bromwyn asked.

Trombone was waiting in the stable; the tack was clean in the kitchen. Nicholas had gone without tea. "If you don't go soon you'll be caught in the thunderstorm. We can't do anything more, it's all done," he said impatiently.

They left at last. Nicholas found bread and cheese and made himself a giant sandwich. Then he started to groom Trombone. While he worked he talked to her. "You're to behave yourself tomorrow, do you hear?" he said. "Jump calmly."

"Hiya," cried Ruth coming into the loose box. "Doesn't the ring look swell. Did you do it all yourselves? It sure looks professional."

"You'll only be able to jump the practice jump. Anyway, you can't do much or you'll make her stale," Nicholas said.

"My, isn't it hot," Ruth exclaimed. "I suppose I'll have to wear my breeches and boots tomorrow or can one ride in a gymkhana in sneakers and jeans?"

"No, one can't," replied Nicholas firmly.

He led Trombone out into the paddock and held the off-side stirrup while Ruth mounted. Thunder muttered and rumbled. It made Nicholas think of his father snoring in a deckchair on Sunday afternoons. People were leaving the beach as though expecting the storm to break.

"I should just ride her round on a loose rein to start with. She's been in the stable all day and needs loosening up."

He found the practice jump and put it up. Drops of rain were falling on his hair. "I shall have to watch the tents," he thought. Ruth was wearing one of her loudly-checked American shirts.

"I suppose you haven't brought a jacket," called Nicholas. She shook her head. She looked well on Trombone. It was extraordinary how much her riding had improved.

She jumped the mare quietly, first from a trot, then from a canter. She couldn't practise much else because the poles and buckets had been stacked ready for the morning.

Ruth's parents were watching over the fence.

"Hi, Nick, you wouldn't like to sell that mare, would you?" her father called. Nicholas shook his head. It was raining now.

"That's enough," he called to Ruth. They settled Trombone, fetching her hay and water and a feed. "Do you want me to braid her mane in the morning?" Ruth asked.

"If you like."

Nicholas felt tired now. It seemed to have been a very long day. He was trying to keep the gymkhana from his mind. He knew suddenly that they had forgotten to find stewards. Who would take the buckets and poles in and out of the ring? "We'll need at least half a dozen," he thought. "When Ruth's gone I'd better start ringing up people."

They all went indoors together and Nicholas thought, "They're never going to go." He couldn't keep the gymkhana from his mind any more and there seemed a mass of things which had been forgotten.

"Nick, what's the matter? Have you gone deaf or something?" Ruth said.

"I can't stop thinking about tomorrow," Nicholas replied.

Like the Fishers, Ruth and her parents left at last, after refusing an invitation to dinner at the Manse.

He wanted to start ringing up straight away but his father was on the telephone making one of those trunk calls which take an age.

Dinner was on the table now and dusk had come. Nicholas felt as though his execution was on the next day.

"I haven't any stewards, no-one even for the car park," he said, spooning curry into his mouth.

"Mr. Jones's farmhand will watch the car park for tips and a pound, I expect. Charge a shilling," his father said.

When Nicholas had helped clear away dinner, he rang the Allcotts' number. Mrs. Allcott answered.

"I don't know where James is. He went out nearly an

hour ago. We're getting quite worried," she said. "It's thundering now; it's going to rain in a moment."

"Perhaps he's sheltering," suggested Nicholas, but he didn't believe it. "More likely he's put his foot in it again somehow or other," he thought.

"Well, we know he isn't with you, anyway," Mrs. Allcott said.

Nicholas replaced the receiver and started to telephone his unhorsey friends. He felt it was cheek but what else could he do? Three of them agreed to be stewards. It wasn't enough but Nicholas had had enough of telephoning and the storm had broken in earnest at last; crashes of thunder drowned words; the gutters were running with water; jagged lightning lit the dusk in sudden savage flashes.

Nicholas tried not to think about James. He stood staring out of the window, knowing that the whitewash would be dissolving into soggy grey puddles beneath the Dog Gymkhana jumps, that the white lines they had marked so laboriously during the afternoon would be gone by the morning, that the peat he had ordered was probably now unnecessary. He went up to his bedroom and switched on his radio. Jazz competed with the thunder. Nicholas lay back on his bed. "Sunday will seem like a holiday if it ever comes," he thought. "Everything will be settled then, one way or the other, for better or for worse. I'd better ring up Mr. Jones in a minute."

He had to struggle against sleep, to force himself to go downstairs, while the thunder was still crashing about his ears, to pick up the receiver to telephone Mr. Jones. He was lucky again. Mr. Jones was certain that his farmhand would watch the car park gate for a pound. Nicholas returned upstairs to wind his clock, to wash, to change into his pyjamas and to fall instantly asleep.

Lights on the Sand

Before James could cross the railway line, he had to let an express pass. It was very quiet when the train had gone; he climbed through the wire, ran down the bank and looked both ways before crossing the rails. Dusk had come; he had no time to spare. All too soon his parents would be anxious, all too soon it would be dark. He was wearing his school mackintosh which was navy blue and wouldn't be seen too easily in the coming darkness. He was half afraid, yet compelled to go on by an urge he couldn't explain even to himself. The sea was grey, with rollers which spat white and angry against the rocks. Any moment, the storm would break. James ran. In his mind was the thought, "Tomorrow all may be over."

He reached the horses' field at last. They were still there. For a moment, he nearly turned for home, then something made him go on down the sandy path through the gate to the cove. The first thing he noticed was lights, lights on the sand; his heart started beating like a sledge-hammer against his ribs.

"So my hunch was right," thought James, "something is happening." Next, he made out the figure of Jim Morgan and, immediately, he began slithering towards the sand dunes. He was cold now somewhere in the pit of his stomach. As he crawled behind the first dune he reached, rain fell on his hair.

"I should have asked Nicholas to come with me," he thought. "What will Jim Morgan do if he sees me here?" There was a ship he saw now, from which parcels were being unloaded. Three men worked in waders and dark mackintosh capes. Jim Morgan put the parcels in a sack, slung it over his shoulder as the other men returned to the boat. Someone called, "Monday then." Jim Morgan's reply was drowned by the first crash of thunder; then lightning lit the sky and the rain came. James lay flat on the sand. He didn't want to know anything more because it was obvious to him that the whole business was illegal. He lay behind the sand dune for a long time. He heard Jim Morgan shutting the gate which led to the beach, he heard him call softly to the horses; then there was complete silence except for the occasional crash of thunder and the sound of the sea and the falling rain.

James stood up at last. His hair dripped water on to his face. His mouth was gritty with sand. It was very dark.

Quite suddenly his teeth started to chatter. After a time, he found the path to the gate. He started to run. Then he saw lights at last and, heading towards them, reached the road. For a moment, he was lost, before he realised that he was outside the riding school. He started to run along the well-known road to home.

Presently a torch was coming to meet him, a voice called, "Is that you, James?" "Hullo, Daddy," he called, staring along the dark, wet road.

"Wherever have you been? Never do it again, James. Don't you realise how anxious we've been?" said Mr. Allcott, for now he had reached his son.

"I'm sorry," James answered. But he wasn't really, not deep down inside. He was filled with jubilation suddenly. "Jim Morgan's a smuggler. I've got proof of it now," he said.

His father took his arm. "You're soaked. Really, James, you're old enough to know better. Do you realise it's nearly ten o'clock? The pubs will be coming out soon That's a fine time to come home on a Friday night," scolded Mr. Allcott.

There was a solitary light showing through the curtains in Jim Morgan's house. "Is he home? Or is his wife waiting up for him?" wondered James. The rain had almost stopped. "Perhaps it'll be fine tomorrow," thought James. He felt like singing, which was ridiculous on such a miserable night.

"How you will get up in the morning I don't know," said Mr. Allcott.

"I have to be at the Manse by six," James remembered.

"At last! I thought something terrible had happened. James, where have you been?" Mrs. Allcott welcomed them. "Here, get your wet things off and into a hot bath with you."

"I'm not sleepy," complained James. "Jim Morgan's a smuggler. He's outside the law."

"You tell me all about it in the morning," replied his mother, already running the bath water.

"They're not really interested," thought James. "I can't tell them in the morning, there won't be time."

The Fishers were the first in the field next morning, closely followed by Ivor. Anne, loaded with canvases, felt half asleep. The sun had risen and everything seemed to point to a perfect day. The grass was wet under their feet and only a solitary dog gambolled alone on the beach. There was no sign of Nicholas.

"I'm going to put up my table and get to work," Anne said. She started to fetch clothes from the green-house.

"Look, all the white lines have gone," cried Bromwyn.

"And look at the Dog Gymkhana jumps," wailed Maria.

Ivor arrived then, in corduroy shorts and patched shirt, with a pen jutting out of his shirt pocket.

"Where's Nicholas?" he asked.

"Still asleep, I suppose," replied Bromwyn.

"Look at the Dog Gymkhana jumps," wailed Maria.

"Have you got a watch, Ivor?" asked Bromwyn.

"No, but it must be six because Mum was just getting up when I left and she gets up at a quarter to."

"Come on, Maria. If we whitewash the jumps again, they'll most likely be dry by the afternoon," he added.

Ivor started to whistle. Maria found the whitewash and brushes. Someone let Watchman, the boxer, out; then

Nicholas called, "Hullo, just coming," from his bedroom window.

"I hung up the CAR PARK notices on the way along," Bromwyn said to no-one in particular.

"Someone help me arrange the pictures. I don't know where to put them; they looked so silly mixed up with the old clothes," Anne complained.

"Why not arrange a separate display next to the stall? We can prop them up with sticks at the back of the canvas. I say, they're not at all bad," exclaimed Nicholas, suddenly beside her.

"Of course, they're good. Daddy's an artist," shouted Maria.

James had wakened to find Jocelyn shaking him. "Do get up, we're late already," she whispered, fully dressed, her pockets bulging with papers. For a moment, James couldn't remember anything; then it all came back.

He was wide awake now. He sprang out of bed. No sign of the storm remained. It was like a spring morning with a bird singing in every tree. James dressed quickly, gulping his tea at the same time. He met Jocelyn on the doorstep.

"Here, eat these as you go along," she said, handing him a packet of sandwiches. "Whatever happened to you last night? I tried so hard to stay awake, but I just couldn't."

"We'd better run," replied James, his mouth full of egg sandwich. "I'll tell you when I tell the others. It'll be quicker that way."

When they reached the showground, everyone asked the same question – "Whatever happened to you last night?"

"How do you know about that?" asked James, flustered and surprised, his hair in his eyes, one sandal strap undone; he was not at all the usual neat figure. He felt apprehensive now and rather disappointed. "How can they know everything so soon?" he wondered.

"I rang up. Your mother told me you were lost. Or was it your father, I can't remember which. Where were you actually?" Nicholas asked.

Stella had just arrived on the early bus, her satchel on her back. She was the only one dressed in the clothes she meant to wear all day. Choosing them had caused her a good deal of agony. Should she wear riding clothes or a frock and cardigan? Her mother favoured a frock but, in the end, at the last moment, Stella put on her jodhpurs and her best shirt. Now she stood wondering why everyone was clustered round James.

She hadn't long to wait.

"I went to see the horses; they're still there; but I found out something very important," James said.

"Jim Morgan's a smuggler. Men were bringing in packages from a boat, whisky or something. I saw it all. We can get him into trouble now, though we mustn't try blackmail. You know, say 'either let us have the horses or else'; but it's a lever all the same . . ." James said.

"Smashing," announced Ivor.

"Was Jim Morgan there then?" asked Bromwyn.

"Of course. Didn't I say so?"

"No."

"He took the packages away in a sack. I hid behind a sand dune. It was pouring with rain and thundering like mad."

Nicholas could feel his envy turning into hostility. "No-one will believe you, they'll want proper witnesses," he said.

"We'll have to fix that up somehow," James replied. "Hadn't we better get down to work. It must be seven o'clock."

He felt he could stand up to Nicholas now. The last few days had changed everything. Before, he had always treated him with certain reverence, now that was past.

"I always knew he was a burglar or a smuggler," cried Maria.

"Good old James!" exclaimed Ivor, slapping him on the back.

Somehow it already seemed James's day. He had brought a collapsible card table and a camping stool which he put up just inside the gate. Nicholas started to tell everyone about the shortage of stewards. "I'll help when my stall's sold out. It's sure to be by lunchtime," Anne said optimistically.

"Daddy says he'll take a turn at the gate," James said.

"I thought parents weren't to help," Nicholas replied.

"Well, your father's judging."

"And Mummy's going to help me if I get in a muddle," Stella said.

Jocelyn was putting her tent in order. She wished she had gone with James last night. It had been awful to creep to bed exhausted, not knowing where he was.

The day was growing hotter now. In the old-fashioned stable yard, Nicholas had tied Trombone to a ring in the stable wall while he cleaned out her loose box.

"Breakfast, Nicholas," his mother called. The help didn't come on Saturday, so today his mother had cooked the breakfast.

"How's it going, Nicholas?" she asked.

"Middling. The storm didn't do any good."

"Anne's table is absolutely covered; she's a wonderful girl," said Mrs. Owen.

"She's not my type," replied Nicholas, who could only find fault with everything.

Presently, he was back in the field working with the others, while Trombone stood munching a feed, washed and groomed, waiting for Ruth to braid her mane.

It was nine-thirty and everything seemed ready.

"We're going home to change," Bromwyn said.

"People will be coming soon. Don't be long," James answered. "Come on, Jocelyn, we'd better rush too."

Ivor had already gone. He was running home. One of his sisters had promised to bring Pete for the flat race.

Only Stella and Nicholas remained and then, presently, a large car swung into the field and Ruth stepped out.

"Am I late? My, doesn't it look wonderful?" she cried.

"We'll come back later," her father called, turning the car.

Ruth was resplendent in breeches and boots, a blue silk shirt and bow tie. She strode across to Nicholas, and, suddenly, it seemed to him that, with her coming, the real business of the day had started.

The Day

Ruth was still braiding Trombone when the first competitors started to arrive. First came a horse box, which sent Nicholas rushing indoors to change into respectable clothes. He felt on edge now. He had lost his megaphone. There was no loudspeaker; no-one had done anything about the music for the musical chairs. "How will anyone hear me calling out the numbers?" he wondered, charging through the Manse calling, "Mummy, Mummy, have you seen the megaphone?"

His father was struggling into riding clothes which he hadn't worn for ten years. "Should have tried these on last night," he muttered.

Mrs. Owen found the megaphone.

"Now don't panic so. It's your besetting sin. There's still plenty of time," she said.

"People are arriving. Miss Prickett will be here soon. Where's Bromwyn?" cried Nicholas. The refreshment people were putting up their tent. He could see James now, sitting by the gate. Jocelyn was handing out numbers to the first competitors. Somehow, the whole affair was beginning without Nicholas, who was still struggling into his grey suit and his suede shoes. He put on his school tie and brown Homburg hat. Looking at himself in the hall mirror he thought he appeared at least eighteen.

Nicholas hurried out. The first villagers were arriving, making a straight line for Anne's stall, with empty, hungry bags and baskets in their hands. He hurried across to the collecting ring and tightened the ropes. The grass was hard and dry under his feet, the sun hot on his hat. James waved from the gate. Anne was saying, "It'll be opening in ten minutes."

People looked at Mr. Fisher's canvases and exclaimed, "Fancy, if that isn't the old slag heap at the back of our place!" and "Five guineas! He's hopeful, isn't he?"

Anne had put on a gay, full skirt and white blouse. She felt completely at home behind the large trestle table loaded with its strange assortment of goods. "Thank goodness it's fine," she kept thinking, "and what a lot of people are coming in. Surely we will make two hundred pounds."

Nicholas and Bromwyn started to arrange the ring for *Class 1*, Handy Pony Competition under ten years. Bromwyn was dressed in a linen frock and grey sandals. "All the notices are up. When do you think Miss Prickett will arrive?" she asked.

"Any time now." Nicholas could see Ruth leading Trombone out of her loose box. "I'm sure it's too early," he thought. "She won't have digested her feed."

An Austin drove past James. "That must be Miss Prickett. I sent her a badge saying 'Judge'," Nicholas said.

"How efficient."

"You'd better look after her; explain what each competitor has to do in the Handy Pony Competition. Here comes my father."

"It's an awful strain," thought Bromwyn. "How wonderful Daddy's pictures look. I hope it isn't too hot for them."

She shook hands with Miss Prickett. "You found the place all right then," she began.

The Dog Gymkhana didn't start until after lunch. Ivor found he had time now to help Nicholas, who was putting up what he called 'horse lines' which was something which had been forgotten.

Maria was showing competitors the water trough and Secretary's tent and preparing to help Anne who was opening her stall in three minutes. Stella was already taking down entries for the Dog Gymkhana, feeling surprisingly calm.

Nicholas looked at his watch and saying, "That's it," to Ivor, hurried across to the collecting ring, picked up the megaphone and called, "Will all competitors for Class 1 come to the collecting ring, please." He felt optimistic now. He thought the paddock really did look like a show ground, that there were enough competitors to make a go of it and that the odds were even on buying the three horses.

Jocelyn put one pound in one envelope, twelve and six in another and seven and six in a third. She labelled them *First Prize, Second Prize, Third Prize,* and put *Class 1* in the top right hand corner of each, before she sealed them. She then found three rosettes, a red, a blue and a yellow and put them beside the envelopes. After that, a competitor came in and said. "Can I enter for the open musical poles, please?"

Jocelyn wrote down her name, the name of her horse and handed her a number. She felt as though she had been doing just this all her life.

"Captain Owen, Miss Prickett," Bromwyn introduced the judges to each other.

Miss Prickett was large and businesslike in a linen suit. She shook Captain Owen warmly by the hand, saying, "I'm sure I know you."

Bromwyn could see that Audrey and the riding school ponies had arrived. Nicholas was still calling competitors into the collecting ring. Anne, unable to bear the impatient villagers any more, had opened her stall. Mr. and Mrs. Barr had arrived and were talking to Ruth, who was astride Trombone.

"I think it's time Class 1 started," Bromwyn said to the judges. In the village, the church clock struck eleven.

By twelve-thirty Anne's stall was empty and Ruth had won third prize in the Handy Hunter, much to the Fishers' and Allcotts' surprise. James estimated that he had taken nearly ten pounds at the gate by this time. Now his father had taken over and James stood with his mother trying to believe that all this was really happening.

"I never thought it would be like this. It's quite a surprise. You have done well, I must say, giving credit where credit's due," said Mrs. Allcott.

It was very hot, without a cloud in the sky, nor a ripple of wind.

"I don't know what Nicholas wants to wear a suit for on a day like this. He must be stifling," continued Mrs. Allcott. "Daft, I call it."

"He looks smart in it anyway," James answered.

Nicholas was announcing a lunch interval until two o'clock. Already there was a queue at the water trough and the refreshment tent was doing great business.

"I've brought a picnic lunch," said Mrs. Allcott.

James called, "Well done, Ruth. Jolly good." Jocelyn put a notice outside her tent which read *Reopening 1:45*. She joined James and Mrs. Allcott, clutching a bag of money.

"There's quite a lot here," she said, "Where shall I put it?"

She felt exhausted now. "I must have a lemonade or something," she said.

"I'll take the money into the Manse for you, James said.

Anne was taking down her trestle table. "I'll be able to help with the stewarding," she thought, before she observed the Barrs looking at her father's paintings.

"My, my," said Mrs. Barr. She was tall and slim, fair and blonde, casually smart and unmistakably American.

Ruth had won third prize in the Handy Hunter

"It would remind us of something. Heck, I like them," exclaimed Mr. Barr. Ruth stood behind her parents holding Trombone. Sweat glistened on her face, her sleeves were rolled up, her boots dusty, her bow tie askew. Anne liked her better suddenly; she seemed less of an outsider in her disarray, more of a kindred spirit.

"I don't like the slag heap. But the seascape's fine," Mrs. Barr said.

Anne thought it like them to choose that one. What had her father said about it? "If any one is sold, it will be that one." "How well he knows people," thought Anne.

"Eight guineas, what's that in dollars?" Mr. Barr was already pulling out a wallet of dollar bills.

They started to add it up, while Anne felt a sense of triumph steal over her. "Daddy will open a bottle of wine tonight," she thought. She took the dollars, saying, "Thank you, Mr. Barr."

"How about you, Ruth. Do you want one?" he asked his daughter.

Ruth pointed at the one entitled 'Old Bedsteads'. Behind the bedsteads rose the mountains.

"I'd sure like that one," she said.

The wallet came out again. "We'll have to cash another cheque tomorrow," said Mr. Barr. "But I think we're on to something good. In ten years, who knows, people may be paying hundreds, thousands of dollars for a Fisher."

Anne's heart warmed to him. Wasn't that what they all thought in the cottage? In a sense, it was the only thing which made life bearable sometimes. "Perhaps this is the beginning," Anne thought, accepting more money, in English notes this time.

Here was Miss Prickett coming across with Nicholas, saying, "I've always wanted a picture by a local artist. It is so much more rewarding to buy an original rather than a reproduction. I mean, you never know, do you?"

Nicholas was trying to hurry her. The judges' lunch had been waiting since twelve-thirty. Bromwyn, who had been invited, was in the kitchen helping his mother dish up.

He felt rather hot and rather cross in his suit, though the show couldn't have been going better.

Murmuring, "So realistic," rather self-consciously, Miss Prickett chose the slag heap. There was only one painting left now. Anne started to regret the ones turned into a wall for the Dog Gymkhana as she took a five-guinea cheque from Miss Prickett's large, damp hand which had made the ink smear.

At last, the judges were seated at lunch. Outside, the gang (except for Nicholas and Bromwyn) put up the jumps for the jumping class for ponies under thirteen two. It was too hot for much conversation but Maria and Anne were jubilant. Ivor's father had arrived with the old greyhound Pete; and his sister Doreen, gay in a floral dress. His mother clutched a pile of garments she had bought at Anne's stall. As Ivor had expected, his father wore his best suit with a watch and chain and dark cap.

Everything was ready in the Dog Gymkhana ring. All sorts of dogs had arrived but Ivor couldn't see one which looked faster than old Pete.

He could see Mrs. Carson now walking across the paddock in a summer dress. "Stella, here's one of the judges," he called panicking suddenly, thinking, "What shall I say?"

"I'll look after her," cried Maria, who, with three of her father's paintings sold, felt herself capable of anything. "And here's Mr. Jones," Ivor added, thinking, "Why must everyone come at once?"

Ivor had been made to wear his best clothes. He felt dressed for Sunday School but was consoled by the fact that Nicholas wore a suit, too, though with long trousers.

Stella and Maria took charge of the judges; they almost fought over them. Ivor found Nicholas's megaphone and started to call Dog Gymkhana competitors into the ring for Class One. The heat was almost unbearable now. The only shade was where the horses stood tied to the rickety lines Nicholas and Ivor had constructed earlier.

Lunch was finished in the Manse. In the stable yard, Ruth was mounting Trombone; they could hear the ring of hoof on cobble even in the dining-room.

The day was almost over now, though people were still coming in at the gate. James took their money and thought about seeing Jim Morgan. It seemed a long time since that first day when the plan of buying the horses had been born. Yet it wasn't long at all, a mere ten days. His head ached from sitting so many hours in the sun. He knew now that he had chosen the dullest job of all but then someone had to do it; who else would have stuck it out? Ivor? But he was too young.

"A shilling please," James said, as footsteps halted by the gate.

"What, full price at this time of day?"

James half recognised the voice, but his mind was still with the Fishers. "Yes. It's for charity, you see. For three horses who are going for meat otherwise," he answered.

He wondered afterwards what had made him say that. He hadn't said it before, not to anyone.

"I know that." James looked round into Jim Morgan's face.

"I just wanted to see how you were getting along, like," he said, handing James a shilling.

James nearly threw the money into Jim Morgan's face. He gave him an icy stare while the words choked in his throat and Jim Morgan walked towards the ring. But a minute later he thought, "It really doesn't matter. He's known all along. He's just come to see whether he's likely to get his two hundred pounds tonight." He decided to leave the gate. Another hour and the whole thing would be over.

Audrey's pupils were cheering by the ring ropes. If things had been normal James would have been there cheering with them. As it was, James was frantic to count the money he had taken at the gate. He saw that Anne was calling to him now and waving.

"My stall made fifty-two pounds five and tenpence," she called.

He shouted, "Well done," and knew suddenly that it wasn't enough, that they weren't going to make two hundred pounds. His throat felt dry. He was stiff from sitting at the gate; his sandals stuck to his hot feet.

In the Dog Gymkhana ring Pete had won the flat race. Doreen was receiving a prize from Mrs. Carson, while Mr. Jones looked on. If it hadn't been for the three horses in the field by the cove James could have been completely happy at that moment. As it was, he was full of nagging doubts.

Nicholas was coming towards him now. Anne was removing the last pole but one from the ring, and James could see that Ruth and the star of the Pony Club, Jane Johnson, were the only two competitors left in the Musical Poles. "I swallow every criticism I ever made of Ruth's riding," James said to Nicholas, "She really does ride well."

The Evening

There was only the Potato Race now in the main ring. The dry earth showed through the parched grass. Anne, Jocelyn, Bromwyn and one of Nicholas's friends put up the poles for the last time, put the potatoes on the top, placed the buckets in line and left with a sigh of relief.

"Am I tired!" Jocelyn said.

"Do you think we'll have enough?" asked Anne.

"You keep saying that," exclaimed Bromwyn.

"I can't help it."

"It's been a howling success anyway," said Nicholas's

friend, a tall youth with ginger hair. "So what are you worrying about?"

"The horses, of course," replied Jocelyn.

"Thank God I haven't got the craze. All this fuss over three cart horses. Have a sense of proportion."

The three girls stared at him in horror. "Have a heart," replied Jocelyn at last.

"A sense of proportion. It's you who hasn't got one," replied Anne.

"Out of the ring, please. The race is starting," yelled Nicholas.

"We're going to hold it every year for good causes," said Bromwyn haughtily, but the youth had ducked under the ring ropes and was gone.

"James is counting his money. His face is very long," Anne related.

"But there are lots of people here," replied Jocelyn.

"I know. But ten only makes ten shillings, a hundred a mere five pounds; lots of them are children," said Anne.

"Whatever shall we do if we haven't enough?"

"I don't know."

"Perhaps the Barrs will come to the rescue."

"It's awful to beg off Americans for English causes."

"We can't be bothered with pride. It's the three horses we have to think of...."

They saw Jim Morgan and Bromwyn cried immediately, "He's come to gloat," while Anne said, "What a strange man he is." Jocelyn looking at him said, "I hate him. I can't help it. I know it's wrong, but I do."

"Have you counted your money yet, Jocelyn?" Bromwyn asked.

"Yes, it's only seven pounds. I can't help it I had to take the prizes out of it. I know now we're not going to have enough. What are we to do?" There were tears pricking behind her eyes. She took her handkerchief from her pocket and tried to stop them trickling down her cheeks for everyone to see.

"At any rate we'll always know we did everything we could," said Anne.

"Don't be silly. We haven't finished fighting yet. Cheer up, Jocelyn," Bromwyn said.

The Open Jumping was finishing in the Dog Gymkhana ring. Ivor stood calling the competitors for the Consolation Race. There were only half a dozen dogs which hadn't won a prize and they had to compete in a bending race. Ivor's parents watched him with pride on their faces. "I never knew he had it in him, not our Ivor," his mother said.

Stella had closed her tent. She had counted her takings at least six times already and she couldn't make them more than one pound five shillings and sixpence. It seemed a very small return for a great deal of trouble. Her mother had checked her addition so she knew that there could be no mistake. She felt unbearably hot in her riding clothes and rather sad.

"Whatever can we do now?" she wondered. "It will have to be something desperate." At that moment Maria joined her. "Do you think we've made enough?" she shouted.

"Ssh. Do you want everyone to hear? Why do you always shout?" asked Stella. "Of course, we haven't. There's not a hope."

Suddenly it was over, the races won, the prizes distributed, the rings empty. Bromwyn shook Captain Owen and Miss Prickett by the hand. "I don't know how to thank you for all you've done," she said and wondered afterwards where she had heard that said before.

Miss Prickett's hand was large and soft, Captain Owen's lean and hard. Bromwyn was hot and tired and very anxious; there was a knot in her throat, a hopeless feeling in her heart and a pit in her stomach.

"Thank you very much," she added.

People were leaving. Ivor stood talking to his parents. Stella was with the Allcotts. Jim Morgan had left, but somehow his presence still leaned against the ring ropes mocking them.

Nicholas was unsaddling Trombone. "You rode her beautifully," he told Ruth. He wondered now why he had worried so much. The Barrs stood waiting for their daughter.

"Sure you won't sell her, Nick?" they asked.

"Yes, quite."

"Not for all the tea in China. Isn't that a saying?"

"That's right." Nicholas couldn't describe how he felt. He should be elated, he knew that. Everyone had called the show a success; they had all admired Ruth's riding and Trombone's performance and the pair had won three rosettes, but he only felt a crushing sense of defeat and the certain knowledge that tonight there was to be a showdown with all the dice on Jim Morgan's side.

Presently, they were all together staring at the litter – all eight of them, James and Jocelyn, Nicholas, the three Fishers, Ivor and Stella. Nicholas felt an almost irresistible desire to put off the meeting he knew they must have with Jim Morgan. He kept thinking, "Something will turn up."

Maria was impatient for home, for her father's delighted face, her mother's obvious pleasure. Stella's mother had gone on the five-thirty bus. "Don't be late. You've had a long day. Do you hear, don't be late. Stella, are you listening?" she had said.

"Yes." But Stella hadn't really been listening; her thoughts had been with the three shire horses, the grey, the bay and the dark brown, which she knew now they wouldn't be able to save, unless someone had a brainwave. Ivor had enjoyed himself running the Dog Gymkhana. At the same time, he couldn't help knowing that they hadn't made enough money to buy the three horses. Because of that, he was sad with the hopeless, resigned sadness of people accustomed to poverty.

Jocelyn couldn't help knowing that they had failed, that the last ten days represented ten days of wasted effort. She was tired from the hot, airless hours she had spent in the tent.

Anne and Bromwyn couldn't be wholly sad because of the pictures which had been sold; at least they had achieved something, had dragged some sort of success out of the miserable plight of the three horses. As for James, he alone still saw adventure ahead, dangerous perhaps but completely necessary. It was as though the challenge of saving the horses had somehow brought him to terms with himself, had given him boundless confidence in himself, so that he could lead, where he had always followed before.

But now Mr. Jones's farmhand was coming towards them.

"I thought I'd find you here. I don't want to take all this money home," he called.

They had forgotten the car park. For a moment all their faces lit up. Then suddenly they knew, to a man, that it couldn't be enough.

The man who stood before them was small and swarthy. "I did my best for you. I'm fond of horses myself; used to work a pair when I was a lad. It's exactly fifteen pounds I've got here," he announced. "How's that?"

It was more than any of them expected, much more, yet it still seemed like a drop of rain in a whirlpool.

"Thank you so much. What about your pound?" Nicholas asked. "Have you taken it out?"

"No, I don't want that, not seeing what the money's for. That's my contribution."

They thanked him and he went away, stepping over the litter, treading heavily in working boots on the worn grass.

"Let's go to my room and count up what we've got," Nicholas suggested. "Mr. Barr gave me some dollars."

Inside the Manse was cool. Nicholas's room was in a

mess. He started to hurl clothes off his bed, to kick espadrilles into a corner. Out of habit, he switched on the wireless and they heard the weather forecast – "More thunder is expected to spread slowly eastwards. There is no sign of the heatwave abating."

"It seems to have been like this for ever," James thought, "I can't remember another summer like it."

They started to count the bags of money. Though they knew it couldn't be enough, they counted it over and over again.

"It's no good seeing Jim Morgan. He'll only mock us," James said. "We'll have to think of something else." He wasn't tired, but keyed up, full of energy, ready for anything.

"Couldn't we buy one anyway?" asked Stella.

"What does it come to exactly?" asked Ivor for the third time.

"Oh, Ivor, not again," cried Bromwyn. "It's nearly a hundred pounds too little."

"It would still buy one; that's better than nothing," replied Ivor obstinately.

"But it's not good enough. We've got to stop the horses going on Monday. There must be something we can do," James said.

"Lots of things," cried Maria, her face lighting up.

"Inside the law," Nicholas said.

"We can let the horses out. Stop the boat coming in, fight Jim Morgan," Maria suggested.

"It's too hot to think of anything tonight. Are we going to buy one horse at any rate?" Nicholas asked.

There was a chorus of "Yes-es."

"Which shall we buy? How much are we going to spend? Who is going to see Jim Morgan?" James asked.

"Not you or Jocelyn. He hates you both," Nicholas answered.

"I've got to catch the seven o'clock bus home," Stella said.

"What about Anne? She hasn't seen him before," Bromwyn suggested.

"Nicholas, Ivor and Anne," James said.

"We'll meet again tomorrow, at the stables, there'll be plenty of tack to clean," James announced. His head was full of wild plans. He saw himself spending the whole of Sunday night among the sand dunes. "Will you ring us later, Nicholas?"

"Okay."

"And we'll ring you, Stella," Jocelyn promised.

They left the money at the Manse. The sun had gone as the Allcotts walked home. Once again a few lingerers were coming up from the beach. There was an air of finality about the evening, as though they had come to the last bridge and had now either to go back or swim through dangerous water.

In the bungalow, tea had long ago been cleared away. Mrs. Allcott got them supper and they ate waiting for the telephone bell to ring, trying not to look out of the window to see what was going on next door.

The Shack Again

The sunlight had gone when they reached the shack but, long before then, they could see Jim Morgan sitting outside, drinking beer.

"I've never been right here before," Ivor said.

"It's pretty ramshackle," Anne answered.

The dogs met them, barking, cringing, running back to their master, while Mrs. Morgan stood shaking mats by the back door.

"Who is going to speak first?" asked Nicholas hesitating. He was wishing now that he had let James come instead, though James would have put his foot in it, doubtless, as he always did.

The clothes-line was hung with tattered underclothes. Leghorn chickens scratched in the dust by the back door.

Jim Morgan raised a hand in greeting. Anne discovered that her heart was beating like a fast-throbbing engine; her hands were sticky and there was a dry feeling in her throat, which made her long for a cool drink.

"You'd better, Nicholas," Ivor said. He wished suddenly that he had brought his father who, in Ivor's opinion, was a match for anybody.

"Which do we want to buy?" Nicholas asked.

"Can we only buy one?" Anne answered.

"It looks like it."

"The grey," Anne replied.

"Yes, the grey," said Ivor.

Jim Morgan was standing up, one hand outstretched. They could hesitate no longer. In a ramshackle shed a cockerel crowed.

"You made a good job of your gymkhana, a very good job." Jim Morgan greeted them.

They didn't want his congratulations.

"We've come about the horses," replied Nicholas coldly.

"Have you brought the money?" Jim Morgan asked with a smile on his lips which never reached his eyes.

"How much do you want for each horse?" Nicholas asked.

"You haven't enough then? You can have the grey for sixty. The other two are seventy apiece," Jim Morgan replied.

"So this is what he expected," thought Nicholas. "He's worked it all out."

"We'll give you fifty for the grey, that's a very fair offer," he answered.

"Nothing doing. If I let you have her I'm letting down a very good friend, you understand. I wouldn't do it normally," Jim Morgan said.

They all felt the same hopeless sense of defeat.

"We'd better buy the grey," Anne said.

"One's better than nothing," Ivor agreed.

"But we've got enough to buy any one of them," Nicholas replied.

He wanted to buy the grey too, because he loved greys, probably because Trombone was a grey, but was that enough reason? he wondered.

"Which is the youngest?" he asked.

"The brown. He's rising five." They all knew now which they would buy. Anne started counting out the money.

"Come inside," Jim Morgan said.

The shack smelt of the oil cooker in the kitchen. Newspapers were spread on the kitchen table in place of a cloth.

"Can we put down twenty-five or thirty on the grey? We'll soon raise the rest," Nicholas asked.

"No, the other two must go on Monday. You're buying the brown then?"

"Yes."

The money was counted at last.

"When can we fetch the horse?" Nicholas asked.

Ivor stood there saying nothing. In a way, he was sorry they had decided to buy the brown, though, of course, it was right, seeing he was only five. He hoped his mother had kept some tea for him. The morning seemed to belong to another life.

"You know where the horses are then?" Jim Morgan asked.

"Yes."

"Still, you don't know how to get to them. I'll bring him round on Monday early to your place."

"We want a receipt please," said Anne, who didn't feel like handing over the money. "Can't we have the horse tomorrow?"

"Not on a Sunday. I'm not going down there on the Sabbath. Day of rest that is."

The children looked at Jim Morgan in amazement

while he wrote on a scrap of paper. When he handed it to Nicholas the boy read, *Received 70 pounds in payment for brown cart gelding rising five*. It was dated and signed, *J. Morgan*.

"What does he care for the Sabbath?" wondered Ivor.

"You'd better have the money when we have the horse. Keep the receipt till then," Nicholas said.

"Oh no. Tonight, that was the arrangement; otherwise no business."

Anne handed Jim Morgan the shopping-bag; the rest she stuffed into her pockets.

They all wanted to be gone now. The whole deal appeared underhand and sordid. It seemed Jim Morgan had had it all his own way.

The dark outside was fresh and welcoming after the fetid air in the shack. None of them spoke. Ivor felt Nicholas had failed them somehow. He, as the eldest, should have stood up to Jim Morgan. Anne was thinking about home. Had her father been told about the pictures yet? Was he pleased? Were they already celebrating in the cottage?

"We'll meet tomorrow then," Nicholas said. He was sick of the whole business. What would they do with the brown on Monday? he wondered. He suspected the gang thought the paddock at the Manse would be free for him; but there was no grazing left there now, not even enough for Trombone. He started to look forward to Wednesday. It would be nice to see his other friends for a change and Ruth would be there to amuse them all with tales of Virginia.

"Goodbye," he called, turning away, running homewards along the road.

Presently Ivor and Anne parted. Anne could see the lights of the cottage now, shining through the conifers.

"See you tomorrow then. What a pity we couldn't buy all three," she said.

"But we're not giving up, are we? We can't give up,"

Ivor answered, looking very young and small in the faint light of the ending day.

"No, we can't. But we're all too exhausted to think of anything now. We'll sleep on it, shall we?"

"Okay, as long as we're not giving up," replied Ivor stubbornly, turning towards the village.

"But they are giving up, everyone is but me and Maria and James," thought Ivor presently, pushing open the garden gate which led to the dustbin and the back door. He could see now that Doreen's young man was sitting in the kitchen. Pete lay outside the back door, his grey muzzle tucked between his paws.

When the telephone rang, James answered. He and Jocelyn had been sitting up, waiting. Jocelyn had dozed but James had been too much on edge, too wound up.

"Hullo, is that Nicholas?" he shouted, picking up the receiver. Nicholas said, "We've bought the brown. He's only four. It's the best we can do." Although James had been expecting bad news, the fact that they had bought only one horse was like a sledgehammer blow between the eyes.

"They've only bought the brown. He's four," he repeated stupidly to his sister who had overheard the news anyway.

"What about the others?" asked James. But Nicholas had rung off. James stood looking at the receiver in his hand, "They're giving up," he thought, "they're all giving up."

He felt weak at the knees and sat down. "They're giving up, Jo," he said.

"I know."

Mrs. Allcott came in then. "Come on, off to bed with you, it's past nine o'clock," she said.

"Okay, Mummy. We'll talk about it in the morning, Jo. I'm not giving up, anyway," James said. His bedroom window was open and he could smell the sea which was to take the bay and the grey shires to their fate on Monday, unless he, James, did something.

Stella had been waiting for a long time for the telephone to ring, sitting up in her pink-spotted pyjamas. Her mother sat beside her, sewing. "Surely I can answer it for you," she said for the third time.

Then, at last, it rang; to Stella's flagging spirits it was like a sudden piercing scream. "Hullo, it's Nicholas here. I'm sure James won't remember to ring you, so I am. We've bought the brown, he's only four. We'll discuss the future of the others tomorrow. O.K?" he asked.

Stella was flattered to be rung by Nicholas. "Yes, thank you, thank you very much," she said.

She put down the receiver. "They've only bought one," she said.

"Yes, I heard. But darling, one is better than none. And you couldn't have tried harder, could you?" asked her mother. "Now off to bed with you, and don't wake up early."

Sunday was fine, unbearably hot, with the tarmac sticky on the way to the riding school, and the unmade road to the Allcotts' bungalow a mass of dust and stones.

Jocelyn and James were the last of the gang to arrive at the riding school. Hot and dusty, in the clothes they had worn to church, they didn't arrive until twelve.

The others had decided everything by then and the tack which had been dirtied the day before was hanging, clean, in the saddle-room.

The yard was quiet because the horses were resting as they always did after a gymkhana. Audrey had just distributed glasses of orange squash. Everyone was tired after their efforts, too tired even for much talk.

"We thought you weren't coming," Bromwyn called.

"Daddy made us go to church. Isn't it awful about the other two horses?" James asked.

"We've decided everything," Nicholas said.

"You're not giving up?"

"No. You're to lead us to the field tomorrow at dawn. We'll let the horses out and drive them across the waste land. We'll take the supposed remains of a picnic with us and leave it scattered by the open gate. You know; an old tin or two, a lemonade bottle and lots of sandwich paper. Do you think we're ingenious? Someone will have to keep driving the horses. Of course, it's only a temporary measure. After that we must appeal to societies like the R.S.P.C.A. for help," Nicholas said.

Listening, James could feel his spirits rising. "Nicholas couldn't have thought of a better plan," he decided. The remains of the picnic left by the gate was a touch of genius, for, obviously, they, local residents, wouldn't picnic only a few miles from their homes.

"The only thing is I haven't found the gate into the field, only the one on to the beach." James replied.

"But there must be one," Nicholas insisted.

"Of course."

"That's all right, then."

Now the Allcotts could smile again and, to them, all the afternoon was suddenly free and peaceful because the plan for the next day was hatched; because now they would be able to sunbathe, do whatever they felt like until dawn on Monday. It was as though a weight had been lifted from around all their necks.

Ivor couldn't stop whistling; the Fishers were smiling and laughing. "The R.S.P.C.A. *must* help," Bromwyn said.

"And there are lots of other societies," Anne added.

Stella had to catch the next bus home, but Maria asked her to spend the night in the cottage. "You can't possibly miss tomorrow just because there are no buses at dawn," she said.

"We'll fix you up with a camp bed," Anne had promised. So Stella was able to go with a light heart. "See you at about six this evening then," she called to Maria as she left the yard.

After all the details were arranged – that the Fishers should bring the sandwich papers, Ivor the tins, Nicholas the lemonade bottle; when they should meet and where – they split up, each going home. They called, "See you at dawn," to one another and hurried along hot roads or dusty tracks to Sunday lunches.

"It didn't matter us being late after all," James said.

"No, they've thought up a super plan."

"I hope six o'clock is early enough."

"It's not light before."

They could smell lunch cooking in the bungalow long before they reached it. Jim Morgan was sitting outside his shack, as usual, reading a paper. The beach below was almost empty.

"We'd better get the telephone to call us. We must be on the safe side," James said, opening the garden gate.

Monday

There was a light moving; it shone on James's face, waking him up; then it moved away. He sat up and he knew it was Monday. The alarm clock was beside his bed; he could hear it ticking, though he couldn't see its hands in the darkness. He found the light switch; the time was four-thirty. He switched off the light, went to the window and looked out. At first, nothing seemed to move; then, as his eyes grew accustomed to the dark, he saw that there was a lamp shining in the Morgan's shack and another light disappearing along the road.

His first thought was, "We're too late." Then, suddenly, he knew what he must do. In less than a minute, he was dressed, struggling with the bolts on the back door, running, down the garden path. The air was crisp and fresh; birds twittered sleepily in trees and he could hear, quite plainly, the gentle lap of the sea below on the deserted beach. He knew the way. Hadn't he gone over it twenty times the night before while waiting for sleep?

There was a goods train rumbling along the line when he reached it and he stood cursing, thinking, "I'd like to kill Jim Morgan."

When the train had gone, James slipped down the embankment and across the line. Now, in the distance, cocks were crowing, and the sky had a faint grey streak in the east.

He had no doubts in his mind as he crossed the golf course. Everything seemed as clear to him as the daylight which would soon come. He didn't even wonder whether he might have telephoned Nicholas, have awakened Jocelyn. He was independent by nature; besides, telephoning would have taken time and there was none to spare. He had reached the last field by now; twice he had fallen over hillocks and his knees were bleeding inside his jeans, but he hadn't noticed. As he had expected, there was a light out at sea. Fortunately there wasn't time to feel frightened. He simply slipped through the wire fence and started to scan the field for horses. The sky was now grey all over, a grey tinged with yellow where dawn was breaking. James couldn't see very far. He started to walk round the field. He found a water trough and the gate by which the gang was to have left the remains of a picnic.

Suddenly it was dawn and he could see that the field was empty.

James started to run towards the gate which led to the beach. He could see that a ship was coming in, gulls screeched overhead and the sand below appeared smooth and very white. He couldn't stop thinking, "The field's empty, they've gone, I'm too late."

Going down the path, he slipped and fell into the sand. Now, yesterday seemed to belong to fifty years ago and Saturday to another century. He reached the beach and the sun was up now, shining over the blue-grey, white-flecked sea. The vista was one he would never forget; like a travel poster come true to life; like a painting, like the winning photograph in a competition. He turned right and into view came James Morgan holding the three horses and the ship coming in. There were large hoof-prints in the sand. James felt nothing but mad, overwhelming rage. "So he's sending the brown too, he's taken our money and he's still selling him for meat," he thought, "that's Jim Morgan for you."

He started to yell, "What are you doing with our horse? You're a thief. You should be in prison," and he hardly knew his own voice. Words came tumbling out of his mouth unbidden. "The police should be here. I'm going to tell them everything," he screamed. All the time the boat was coming in, dawn was turning into day, and in the sky the gulls were screeching as though in sympathy.

He ran across the sand with no idea of what he meant to do, possessed by blind rage. The grey mare was resting a leg, the brown and the bay stared at him with surprised, shocked eyes. Slowly, Jim Morgan roped the horses together. Then he came towards James, his feet moving stealthily across the sand.

"So that's what you think of me, is it?" he said facing James. "Well, I'm having you up before the magistrates for crossing the railway line. Haven't you read the notice? I'm claiming the five pounds reward and my mate coming in will be a witness. That's how it will be."

"I'm taking the brown. He isn't yours any more," James said. His mouth was dry now. What would his father say if he was taken to court, he wondered? Then he didn't care. Let Jim Morgan claim the five pounds. What did it matter in comparison with the theft of a horse? He started to untie the brown. He was ashamed because his hands were shaking, but it was with rage he decided – not fear.

Then Jim Morgan was holding him by the shoulder,

"He's taken our money and he's still selling him for meat"

spinning him round; the boat was by the sand dunes with a gang-plank lowered; the gulls were screeching more than ever and James felt a sudden cold rush of fear.

"Now listen, young gentleman. You keep your nose out of my business, understand? I can be nice and I can be nasty. I'm not sending the brown away. I didn't want to leave him up there by himself, that was all. You mind your own business and I'll mind mine. Understand?"

James said nothing. He felt only intense loathing for Jim Morgan. It was a stronger feeling than he had ever felt before.

"What's the trouble, Jim?" called a man from the boat.

"This boy's causing trouble."

"Well, we know how to deal with him, don't we? We can fix him so he doesn't remember anything. Make it look like something else."

"Here's a bag of the stuff, there's two more. Then we'll get the horses on," the man continued.

He sounded in a hurry, which wasn't surprising since day had come. For the first time, James wondered about the rest of the gang. Were they, for instance, waiting for him? Or wasn't it six yet? How long would they wait? Jocelyn must guess he had gone ahead. He started to shiver, though the morning was warm. He suddenly knew he had taken on too much; that he should have telephoned Nicholas before leaving the bungalow.

Now the sacks were lined up on the sand. The man from the boat took hold of the grey mare. "She's the quietest, is she?" he asked.

The cove seemed, suddenly, very lonely, for James knew now that he had reached the moment when he had to act. Jim Morgan was watching him.

The sea was streaked with gold from the morning sun.

"Come on, gid up," said the man and the grey moved forward.

James made a quick decision. He turned and ran up the sand dunes behind him, picking up stones as he went.

Then he stood up and started to throw. The first one hit the man from the boat, the second flew past the mare's ears, the third hit the bay.

Someone started to shout from the boat, "Get that boy," yelled the man leading the grey. "Go on, Jim. We'll never load as long as he's up there pitching stones."

James started to dodge from sand dune to sand dune and then from rock to rock, still throwing stones. More men were coming in from the boat now and their voices were scared.

"Get him, Jim, silence him," they yelled.

The three shires stood with their ears straight up; then the brown neighed and a hand was clapped over his nose. There were four men now on the rocks. James knew his time was running out. He looked round desperately for help, but there wasn't any. He hurled more stones and then started to dodge for his life. Now, sweat was running down his face, his clothes clung to his body, and his legs felt weak like string. They would fix him so he wouldn't remember. What did they mean by that? It was like a nightmare, suddenly, a nightmare without an end. Above, the gulls were still screeching and the sky was clear and cloudless.

He started to slip, to make mistakes. Before, he had jumped from boulder to boulder like a goat, now his breath came in gasps. Then, suddenly, he was cornered. There were men on all sides, all staring at him with a mixture of fear and hate which made his blood run cold. Afterwards, he couldn't have said who grabbed him, but he knew it was Jim Morgan who raised a fist, so that, for a moment he saw the ginger hairs which grew on it, before it met his chin, and he pitched forward into nothingness.

Jocelyn stood alone shivering in the dawn. She didn't know how to tell the rest of the gang what had happened. Now, Nicholas was coming along the road.

"Hullo. Where's James?" he called.

"Gone."

"Gone?" called the Fishers, approaching from the other direction with Stella.

"Gone?" echoed Ivor breaking into a run.

They were all early and James had gone. "Whatever is he thinking of?" shouted Nicholas.

"He's the only one who knows the way," shouted Bromwyn.

"Something must have happened, I'm afraid," Jocelyn said. Looking at her, they saw suddenly how white and pinched her face was in the dawn. "I heard him leave; it was a long time ago. It didn't really register; then, when the clock went off in his room, I waited for him to get up. Later the telephone rang, as arranged, and I found he wasn't there. I haven't told Mummy and Daddy. It was dark when he went along the passage," Jocelyn finished, "Pitch dark."

"Oh Lord," said Nicholas. "Does anyone know the way?"

They stood and looked at one another. Dawn was breaking and it was to be another perfect day.

"I think I know it more or less," Jocelyn said.

"Okay. You go. I've got other plans. I'm going for help," Nicholas answered.

"You think something's happened to him?"

"I don't know."

"Jim Morgan's bicycle isn't in its usual place. I had a look," Jocelyn said.

"Do you want anyone with you, Nicholas?" Bromwyn asked.

"No thanks. Godspeed and good luck."

Jocelyn started to run. She wasn't fast, was always last in the school sports. Her spectacles were clouded with a sudden rush of tears. "Supposing James is dead?" she thought.

Ivor thought, "We're going to be late. We should have met earlier."

"If only we had a gun," thought Maria.

"What help will Nicholas get?" wondered Anne.

Now they were on the golf course.

"We have to cross the railway line. It's illegal," Jocelyn explained.

"Never mind," replied Bromwyn.

Meanwhile, Nicholas was rapping on the policeman's door. At last, it was opened by Constable Wilson.

"I need help," Nicholas said and started to explain.

"That sounds like Smuggler's Cove," said the constable, when Nicholas had finished. To the boy's relief, he took him seriously.

"I'll ring through to Johnstown and get the patrol car to pick us up. Jim Morgan's got a criminal record. He could be up to all sorts of tricks."

While the constable was gone, Nicholas stood wondering why they hadn't approached the police before.

"Now we'll trot along the road and meet them. Come on, son," Constable Wilson said, struggling into his tunic as he ran down the path to his front gate.

The day had come.

The police in the patrol car called, "Hop in." The doors flew open and Nicholas wondered what Constable Wilson had said. Had the police been waiting for this opportunity all along?

"Tell us about the cove," the Inspector said.

"I've never been there. But it's shaped like a horseshoe and hard to find."

"It sounds like Smuggler's Cove, sir," Constable Wilson replied.

"Do you know our best approach?"

"There's only one; the left turn after Sunbury fork. It's little more than a lane, sir."

"I'm afraid James Allcott may be hurt, sir," Nicholas said. "He went down there alone."

They were bumping over stones now. Below them, lay the sea, silver, rose and gold beneath the morning sun.

"Most likely they'll be gone by now," the Inspector said.

They climbed out of the car and started to run across an empty field. "This is where the horses were, I think," Nicholas said.

The sun was in their eyes and they could smell the sea; above them, gulls wheeled screeching.

"We'll be too late," the Inspector said.

"Look there's the gate," cried Nicholas. He had raced the other members of the gang but now, suddenly, he was filled with a sense of futility.

"There are plenty of marks in the sand," cried Constable Wilson, flinging open the gate.

The other constable had a small ginger moustache; the Inspector was a great hulk of a man.

They slid and slipped down the sandy path and, all at once, the cove was in front of them; they saw the ship, the one shire horse which refused to load, Jim Morgan and three men.

"We've got the blighters," muttered Constable Wilson.

The Inspector issued quick, quiet instructions; the police broke up. "Where's James?" wondered Nicholas. He didn't know whom to follow. It was all intensely exciting. "I wouldn't mind being a policeman," he thought.

The men saw them when they were fifty yards away. They left the bay horse looking surprised on the beach and started to run for the ship.

Everybody was running now but there was no sign of James.

Nicholas could hear the gang coming down the path from the field.

"Hullo," they called. "What's happened? Where's James?"

"I don't know. The police are here," Nicholas said.

He felt a leader again. "We'll have to look for him," he said.

The police were dragging the men on to the shore, handcuffed. Jim Morgan cringed, cajoled. "It was all above board, Inspector," he whined.

"Where's the whisky?" the Inspector asked.

The men were unshaven. "That boy! If it hadn't been for him you'd never have had us, Inspector," one said.

Then, behind them, they all heard a cry, "Help!"

"That's James," cried Jocelyn.

The policemen started to shake Jim Morgan.

"What have you done with the boy?" they shouted.

"We'll look," said Ivor.

They started to search the rocks; then Stella cried, "There are sacks here," and the Inspector hurried across, saying, "That will be the whisky."

And, presently, they found James with his hands and legs bound, a black eye and a swollen chin. "At last," he said. "I thought you were never coming. Have you saved the horses?"

"Yes," Nicholas said. "The police are here. Everything is under control."

"I seem to have been here hours," said James as they untied him.

"We'll want a statement from you later on," the Inspector said. "You've done a great job."

"I threw stones at the horses to frighten them. It was an awful thing to do really," related James, rubbing his wrists.

"We've been wanting these men for some time but we could never pin anything on them. Now, we have all the evidence we want, thanks to you," the inspector explained.

"If only we had known that before," sighed James.

"What about the horses?" asked Bromwyn. "One of them is ours."

"We'll see to them. You come along to the police station later on, when you've had some breakfast and a wash," the inspector answered.

There was an air of finality about everything. Jim Morgan was caught, would probably go to prison. "But what about the horses?" wondered James.

"Can you get back all right? We're going to be rather busy for the next couple of hours. There's a lot to be seen to. I'll send a car to pick you up, at about eleven," the Inspector said.

"Send it to the riding school," Nicholas answered.

They felt no triumph; they were too tired; suddenly tired and hungry. James's head ached. It hurt to open his mouth.

"What about you, son? Are you all right?" Constable Wilson asked him.

"We'll radio for the van; then we can take the kids home," the Inspector said suddenly. He smiled in a way which told them that he had children of his own at home, probably still asleep.

"Smashing," muttered Ivor.

Constable Wilson stayed with the horses; the rest of them climbed the path to the field with the sun warm on their backs, the whole day before them.

"This is the end really," decided Stella. "We've won somehow, the horses won't be exported now." Suddenly, the moment was one of the happiest in her life and she started to smile.

"We've won," she said to Maria.

"I know. Jim Morgan's going to prison. But James is the hero really," Maria answered.

"I was right to fetch the police. We should have done it days ago," thought Nicholas.

Brushing sand off her skirt, Anne thought life would seem dull from now on. Then, she remembered that Ruth's father had suggested an exhibition of Mr. Fisher's paintings in New York and the future was suddenly bright with hope.

Bromwyn turned to Nicholas with a smile. "Are you going to America to see Ruth?" she asked. "Because we're probably going too, because Daddy's going to have an exhibition. Mr. Barr came to see us last night."

They had reached the police car now; it was somehow too black and shiny for the rough lane.

The inspector picked up the receiver inside and started to speak. James turned away and was sick on the side of the bank among some nettles; then, to his surprise, he felt better.

The Three Horses

Some time later, they were all together in the police-station. Outside, the heat was blisteringly hot. They felt in a holiday mood. Earlier, climbing into the police car, Nicholas had said, "I'm going to stay in Virginia next summer, it's all settled."

"And Daddy's going to have an exhibition," Bromwyn had answered.

"And none of us liked Ruth at first, not much anyway," Jocelyn had remembered.

The police-station was cool. Ivor couldn't help remembering boys he knew who had been taken there by force. He felt vastly superior. "We've broken a smuggling racket," he said.

Of course, they couldn't forget the three horses. When they had told the police all they knew, James said, "Now what about the horses." It was still an effort for him to speak. His black eye was turning yellow and he couldn't see very well because of it. Everybody was treating him as a hero though, in his own mind, he had only done what any of the others would have done in the circumstances.

"Well, they *do* rightfully belong to Mr. Morgan," the Inspector replied. "I should go along and see his wife. I'm sure she will be open to any offer, poor woman. He's likely to be inside for several years this time."

The police car took them back to the riding school.

From there, they walked, all of them together, to the Morgans' shack. They were too gay to notice the heat. Ivor couldn't stop whistling.

"We'll hold a show next year in aid of something else, won't we?" Stella asked.

"Of course," replied Jocelyn.

Mrs. Morgan was sitting, where Jim Morgan had sat so often before, in front of the shack. She was reading the paper just as he had done.

"Hullo, dearies," she called as they came up the path. "What a lot of visitors I have."

She wore old bedroom slippers on her feet and her hair was scraped back into an untidy bun held together with pins.

"You've come about the horses, I expect," she said.

"That's right," replied Nicholas.

"You can have them all for a hundred and fifty pounds and it doesn't matter when you pay. I'm keeping the money for when Jim comes out; he'll need something then," said Mrs. Morgan.

"We've got more than a hundred now," Jocelyn answered.

"I trust you, dearie."

"We're going to find them good homes," Bromwyn said.

"That's right, dearie."

Somehow, Mrs. Morgan seemed only half alive, as though part of her was already with Jim in prison.

"Can we keep them here while we find them homes?" James asked.

"Yes."

"We've already paid seventy pounds for the brown. I have the receipt," Nicholas said.

"That's all right, dearie."

"We'll bring them here after lunch then," James said.

They left Mrs. Morgan still sitting idly in front of her shack.

They talked to them for a long time

"Now we must find homes for the horses," James said.

"That shouldn't be difficult. We can advertise them in *Horse and Hound* at a nominal price," Nicholas answered.

"I feel so funny. I can't believe it's all over, that we've won," said Bromwyn.

In the cool of the evening, they fetched the three shire horses and led them to Jim Morgan's field in the gathering dusk. They talked to them for a long time.

"Now we can get to know them," James said.

"And give them names. They're smashing, aren't they?" Ivor said, dwarfed by the size of the three horses.

Standing there, they were all at peace with the world. They couldn't put into words what they felt but it was as though they had been swimming in rough seas for a long time and had reached calm waters at last.

"But for us they would be on their way to an abattoir by now," Jocelyn thought, offering the grey mare a handful of grass.

"We'll have to do something about her fetlock. I'll see if Mummy's got any antiseptic," James said.

Later, the gang split up and they went to their separate homes to relate again the adventure of the day. But, whenever Jocelyn and James looked out of the bungalow windows, they could see the three shire horses grazing contentedly in the field next door.

"We'll miss them when they've found homes," James said.

"By that time we'll have found something else to save," replied his sister.

STRICTLY FOR PONY-LOVERS

Now you have finished this novel you know what an excellent story-teller Christine Pullein-Thompson is. She really makes her characters come alive! And the horses – well, they're almost like people (only nicer!)

Dragon Books have published six of her novels. Three of them, *The First Rosette*, *The Second Mount* and *Three To Ride*, make up an exciting series dealing with the adventures and misadventures of David and Pat.

David's whole life is bound up with horses, and his one great ambition is to ride for England. Things go wrong, of course, and at times he even thinks of giving up his dreams and taking an ordinary job like anyone else. But Pat believes in him and he has other friends, besides his ever-loyal animal companions.

Can he achieve what he has dreamed of for so long? Will he wear the British colours? Read the stories and you'll find out!

The Empty Field is also about ponies, only here the real heroes are three beautiful shire horses, condemned to be shipped abroad for slaughter.

The pony-lovers from the local riding school form a gang, and the story tells how they endeavour to thwart the ruthless smugglers who want to steal the horses. There are thrills galore in this book, for all who love ponies and adventure.

You can find out how to obtain these wonderful books, and a lot more, on the next page.

PONY BOOKS are very popular with boys and girls.
Dragon Books have a fine selection by the best authors to choose from:

SPECIAL DELIVERY	Gillian Baxter	35p	☐
PANTOMIME PONIES	Gillian Baxter	35p	☐
SILVER BRUMBY'S KINGDOM	Elyne Mitchell	30p	☐
SILVER BRUMBIES OF THE SOUTH	Elyne Mitchell	30p	☐
SILVER BRUMBY	Elyne Mitchell	30p	☐
SILVER BRUMBY'S DAUGHTER	Elyne Mitchell	30p	☐
MY FRIEND FLICKA PART 1	Mary O'Hara	30p	☐
MY FRIEND FLICKA PART 2	Mary O'Hara	30p	☐
GREEN GRASS OF WYOMING 1	Mary O'Hara	25p	☐
GREEN GRASS OF WYOMING 2	Mary O'Hara	25p	☐
GREEN GRASS OF WYOMING 3	Mary O'Hara	25p	☐
THUNDERHEAD 1	Mary O'Hara	25p	☐
THUNDERHEAD 2	Mary O'Hara	25p	☐
THUNDERHEAD 3	Mary O'Hara	25p	☐
FOR WANT OF A SADDLE	Christine Pullein-Thompson	30p	☐
IMPOSSIBLE HORSE	Christine Pullein-Thompson	30p	☐
THE SECOND MOUNT	Christine Pullein-Thompson	25p	☐
THE EMPTY FIELD	Christine Pullein-Thompson	35p	☐
THREE TO RIDE	Christine Pullein-Thompson	35p	☐
THE PONY DOPERS	Christine Pullein-Thompson	35p	☐
A SWISS ADVENTURE	Pat Symthe	25p	☐
A SPANISH ADVENTURE	Pat Symthe	25p	☐

All these books are available at your local bookshop or newsagent, or can be ordered direct from the publisher. Just tick the titles you want and fill in the form below.

Name ....

Address ....

....

Write to Dragon Cash Sales, PO Box 11, Falmouth, Cornwall TR10 9EN. Please enclose remittance to the value of the cover price plus. UK: 18p for the first book plus 8p per copy for each additional book ordered to a maximum charge of 66p. BFPO and EIRE: 18p for the first book plus 8p per copy for the next 6 books, thereafter 3p per book. OVERSEAS: 20p for the first book and 10p for each additional book.
Granada Publishing reserve the right to show new retail prices on covers, which may differ from those previously advertised in the text or elsewhere.